FUN MONEY
SAVINGS
CHALLENGE
AF487971
COLORING
ACTIVITIES

THANK YOU
THANK YOU
linktr.ee/
CloudIXStudio

Saving for:

Start date:

Finish date:

Goal = $15

Saving for:

Start date: Finish date:

Goal = $20

Saving for:

Start date: Finish date:

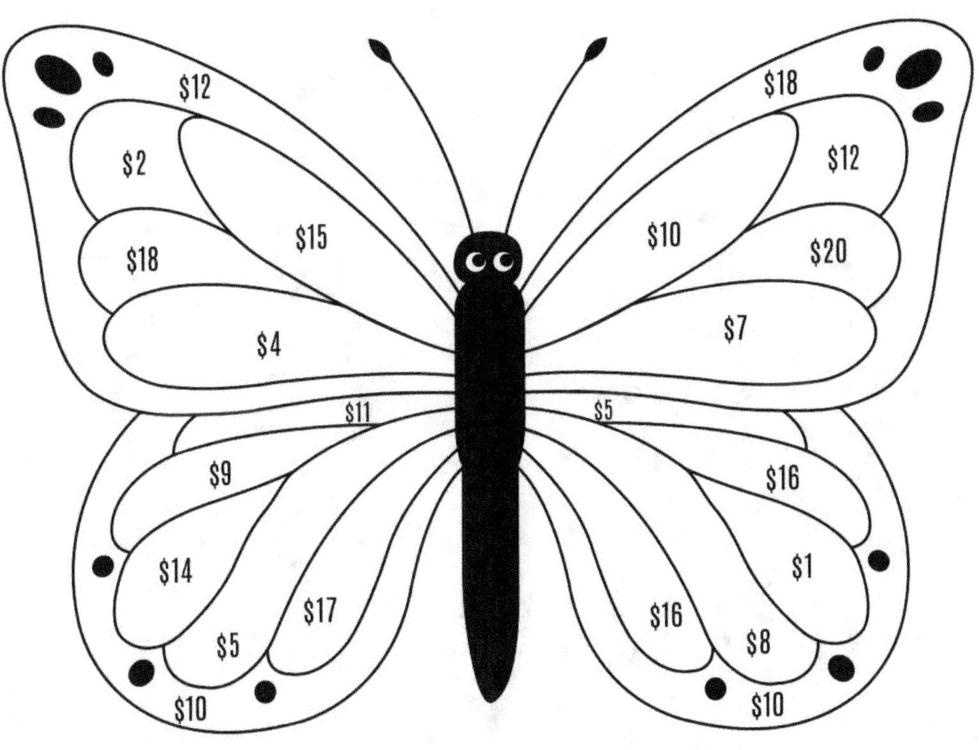

Goal = $240

Saving for:

Start date: Finish date:

Goal = $30

Saving for:

Start date: Finish date:

Goal = $195

$13

$11 $11

$15

$15

$13 $13 $15

$11

$15 $15 $13

$11

$13

$11

Each Cookie = $20

Goal = $300

Saving for:
Start date:
Finish date:
$9
$9
$9
$9
$9
$9
$9
$9
$9
$9
Goal = $90

Saving for:

Start date: Finish date:

$4 $4 $4 $4

$4 $4 $4 $4

$4 $4 $4 $4

$4 $4 $4 $4

$4 $4 $4 $4

Goal = $80

Saving for:

Start date: Finish date:

Goal = $130

Saving for:

Start date: Finish date:

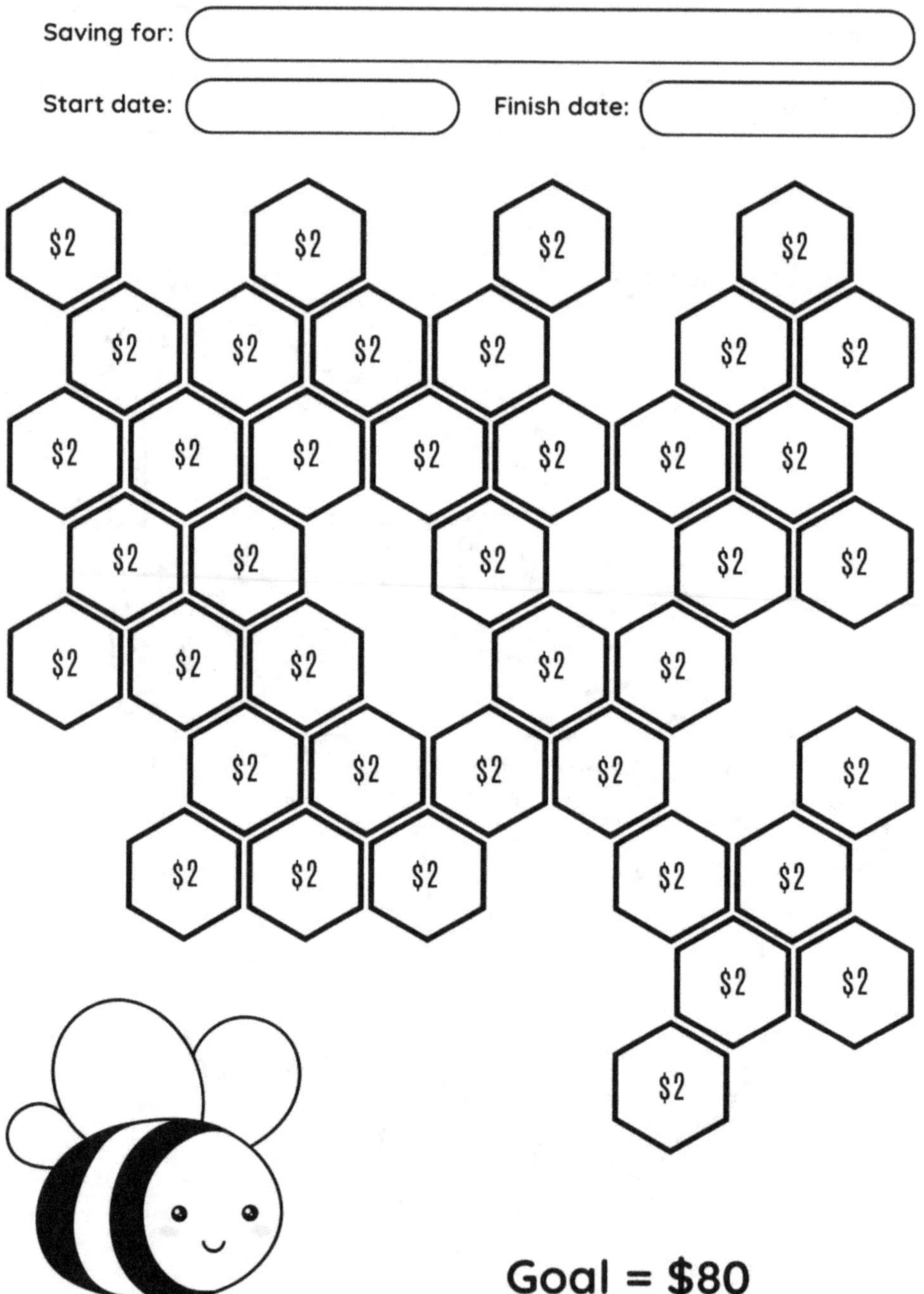

Goal = $80

Saving for:

Start date: Finish date:

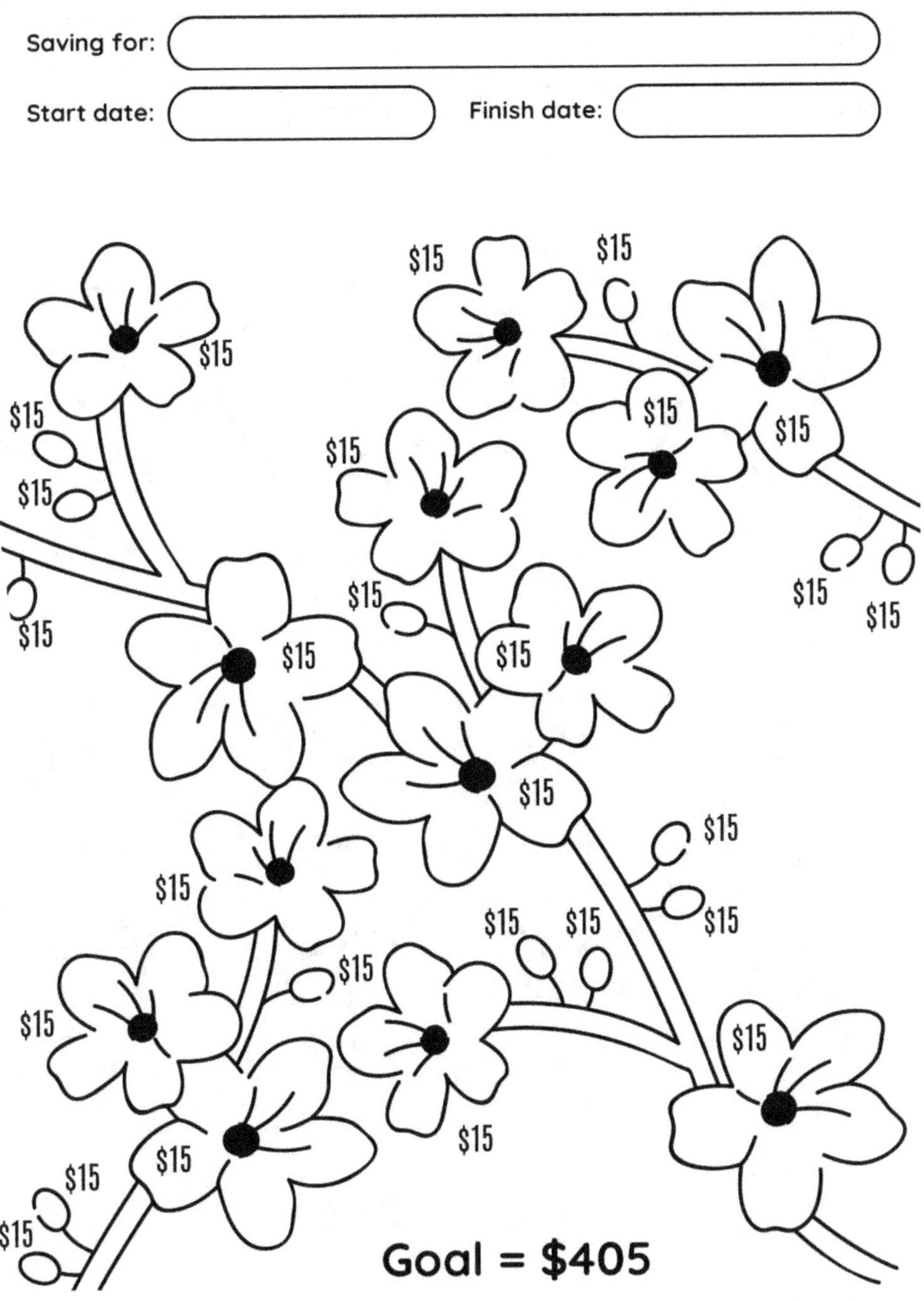

Goal = $405

Saving for:

Start date: Finish date:

Goal = $240

Each Emoji = $20   Goal = $220

Saving for:

Start date: Finish date:

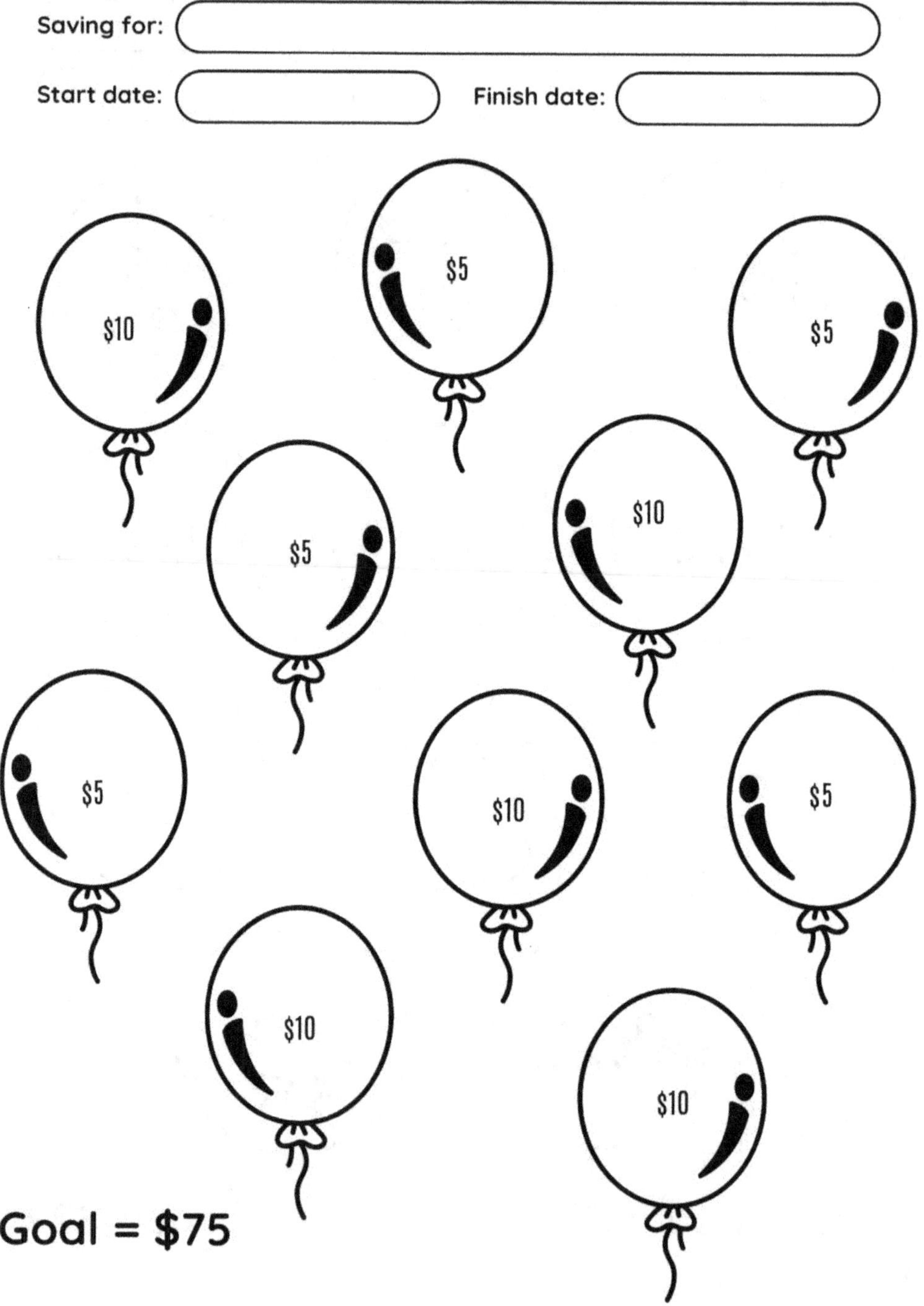

Goal = $75

Saving for:

Start date: Finish date:

Goal = $78

Saving for:

Start date: Finish date:

Goal = $390

Saving for:

Start date: Finish date:

$3 $3 $3 $3 $3 $3

$3 $3 $3 $3 $3 $3

$3 $3 $3 $3 $3 $3

$3 $3 $3 $3 $3 $3

$3 $3 $3 $3 $3 $3

$3 $3 $3 $3 $3 $3

Goal = $90

Saving for:

Start date: Finish date:

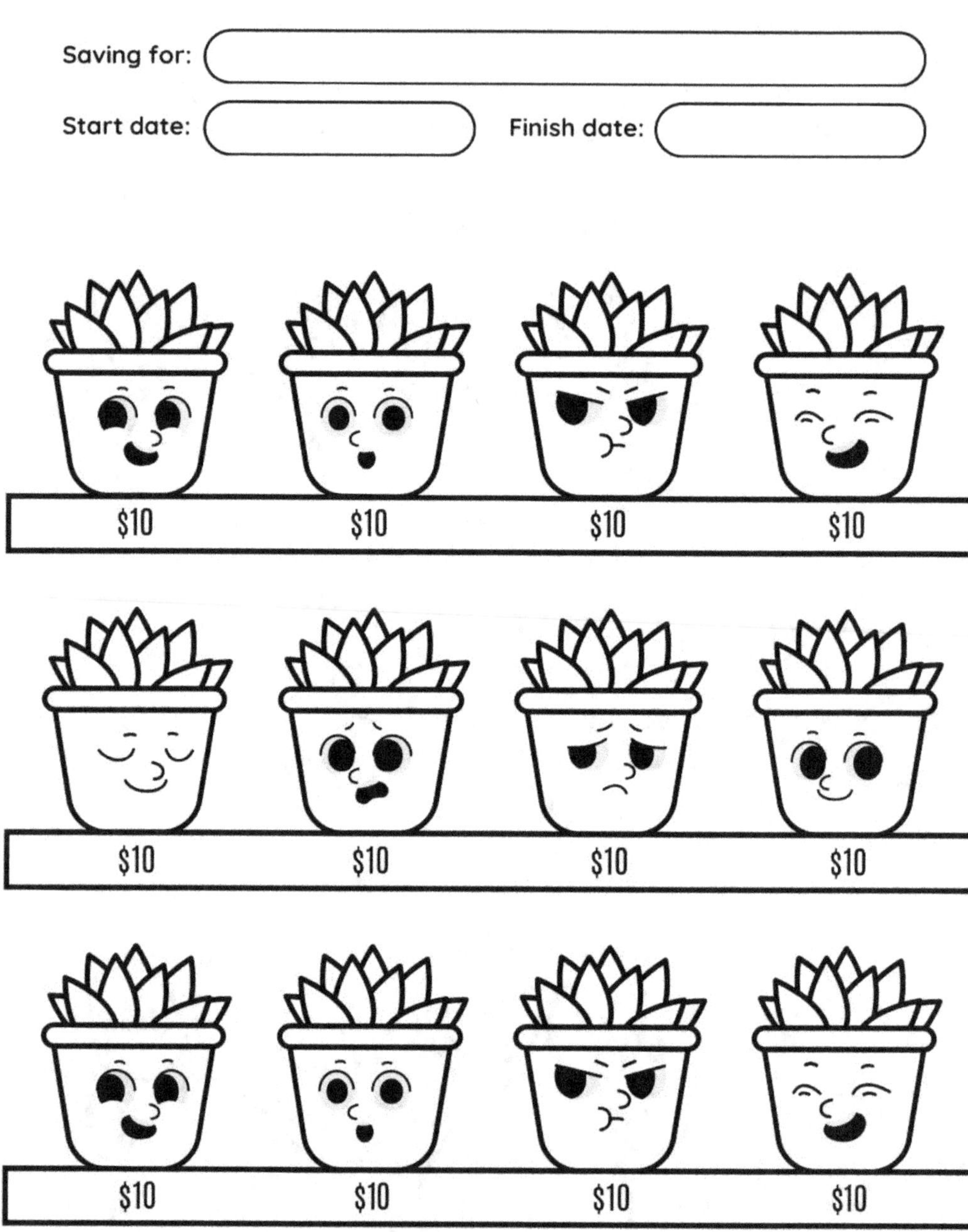

Goal = $120

Saving for: ____________________

Start date: ____________________   Finish date: ____________________

Goal = $85

Saving for:

Start date: Finish date:

Goal = $130

Saving for:

Start date: Finish date:

Goal = $64

Saving for:

Start date: Finish date:

Goal = $75

Saving for:

Start date: Finish date:

Goal = $60

Saving for:

Start date: Finish date:

Goal = $120

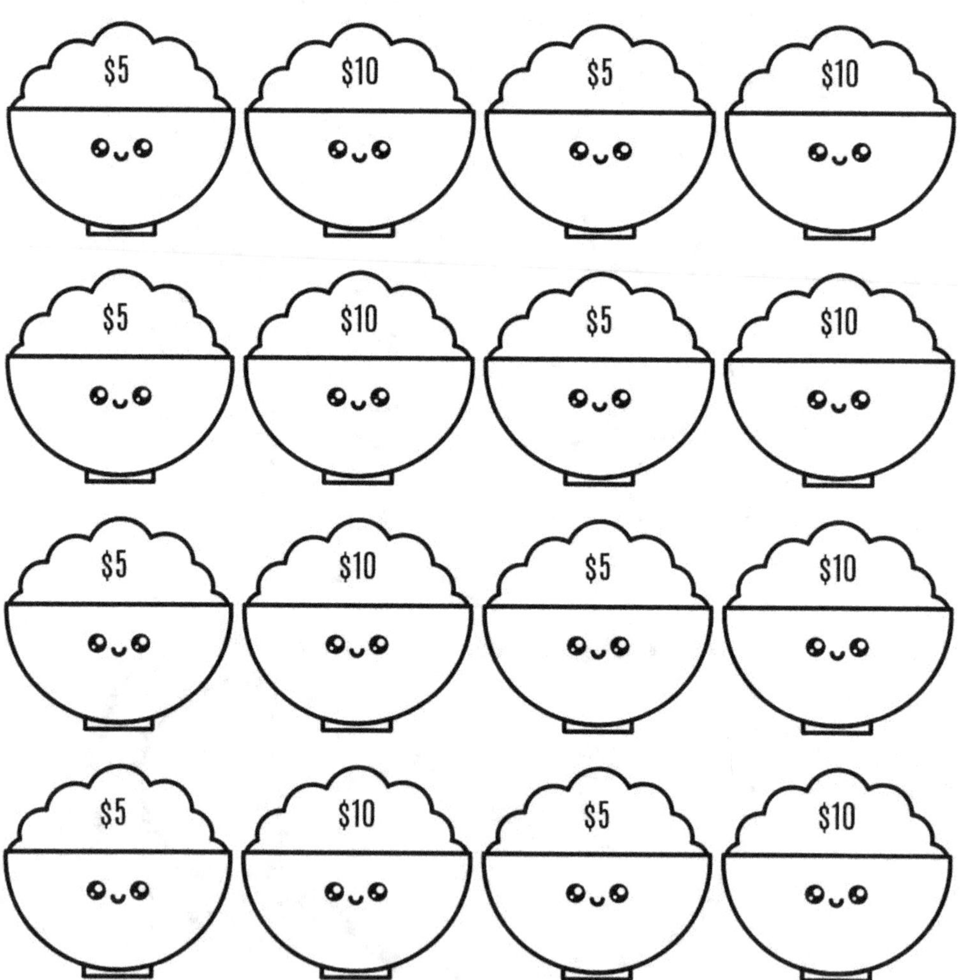

Saving for:

Start date:

Finish date:

Goal = $140

Saving for:

Start date: Finish date:

Goal = $200

Saving for:

Start date: Finish date:

Goal = **$462**

Saving for:

Start date: Finish date:

Goal = $375

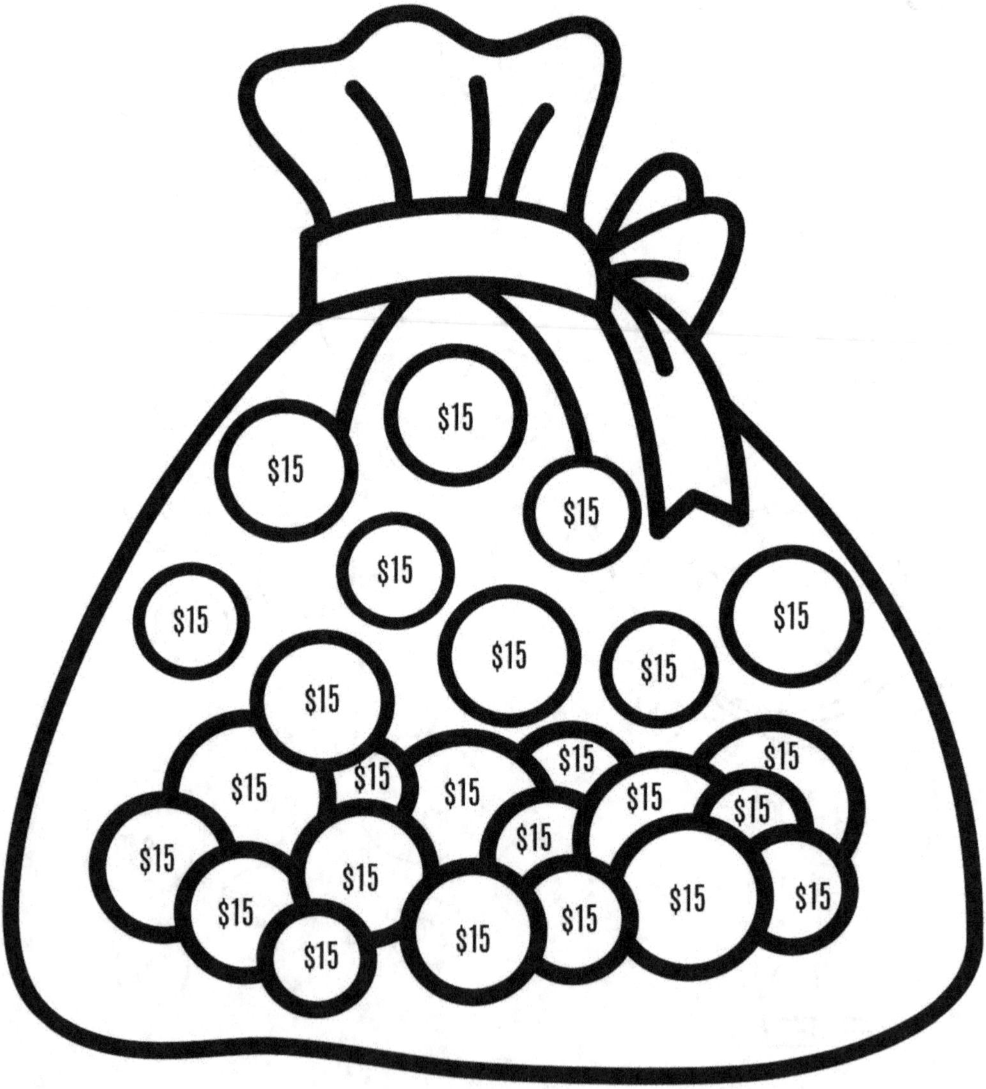

Saving for:

Start date: Finish date:

No Spend Challenge

⭐ = _______________

Total:

Saving for:

Start date: Finish date:

Goal = $750

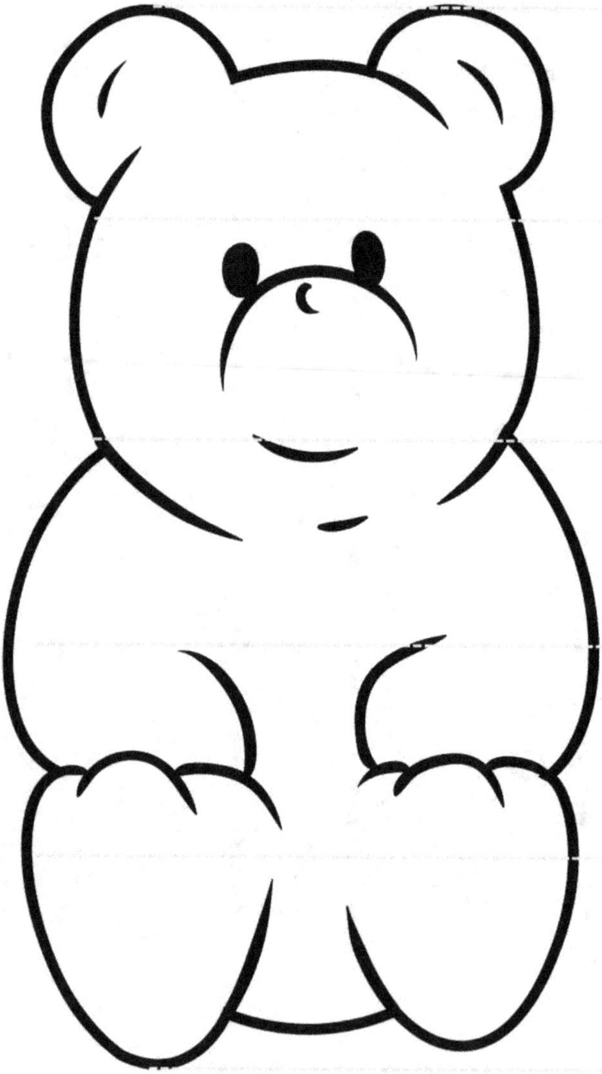

$250

$200

$150

$100

$50

Saving for:

Start date: Finish date:

Goal = $300

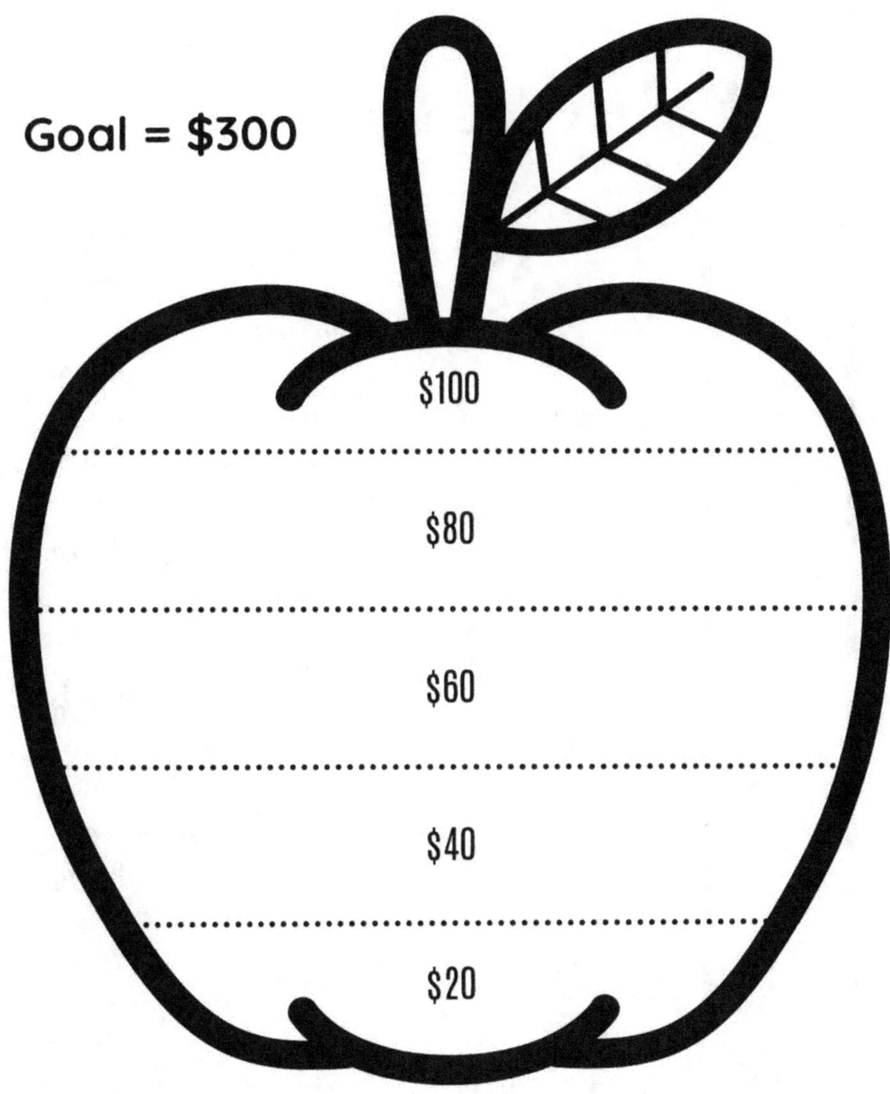

Saving for:

Start date: Finish date:

Goal: ______

100%

90%

80%

70%

60%

50%

40%

30%

20%

10%

Saving for:

Start date:

Finish date:

Goal: _______

100%

90%

80%

70%

60%

50%

40%

30%

20%

10%

Saving for:

Start date: Finish date:

Goal: _ _ _ _ _ _

100%

90%

80%

70%

60%

50%

40%

30%

20%

10%

Saving for:

Start date: Finish date:

No Spend Challenge

☐ = ____________

Total:

Saving for:

Start date: Finish date:

$6 $6 $6 $6 $6 $6 $6 $6 $6 $6 $6 $6 $6 $6 $6 $6 $6 $6 $6 $6 $6 $6 $6 $6 $6

Goal = $150

Saving for:

Start date: Finish date:

No Spend Challenge

= ________________

Total:

Saving for:
Start date:
Finish date:
$20
$20
$15
$5
$10
$5
$5
$10
$15
$10
$15
$5
$5
$10
$15
$10
$5
Goal = $180

Saving for:

Start date: Finish date:

No Spend Challenge

◇ = ________________

Total:

Saving for:

Start date: Finish date:

Goal = $210

Saving for:

Start date: Finish date:

Goal = $280

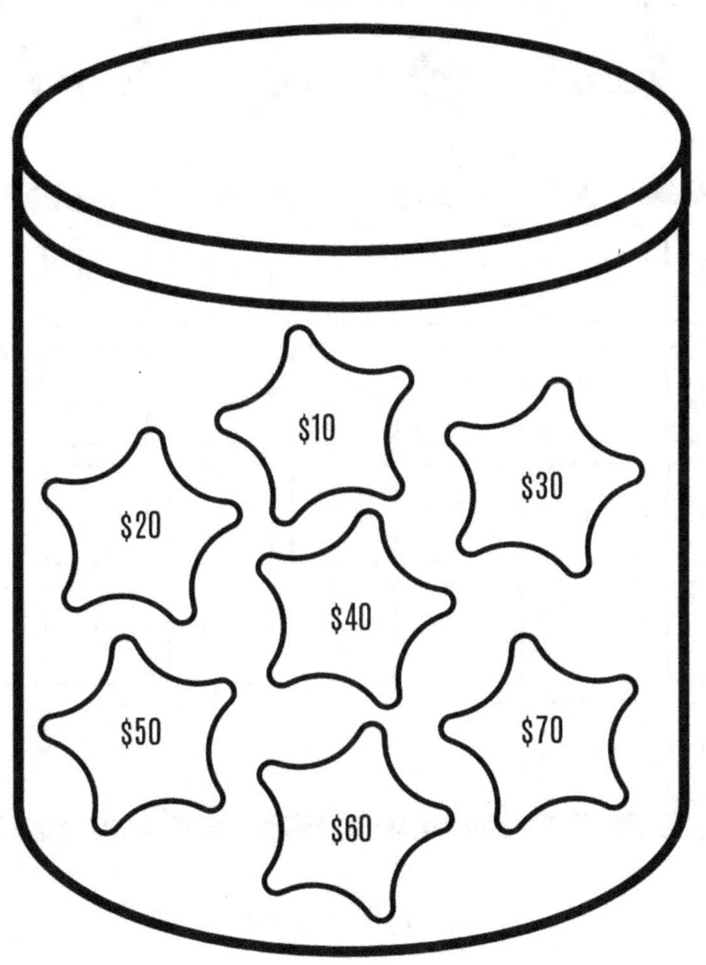

Saving for:

Start date: Finish date:

$10 $10 $10 $10 $10 $10 $10
$10 $10 $10 $10 $10 $10 $10
$10 $10 $10 $10 $10 $10 $10
$10 $10 $10 $10 $10 $10 $10
$10 $10 $10

Goal = $310

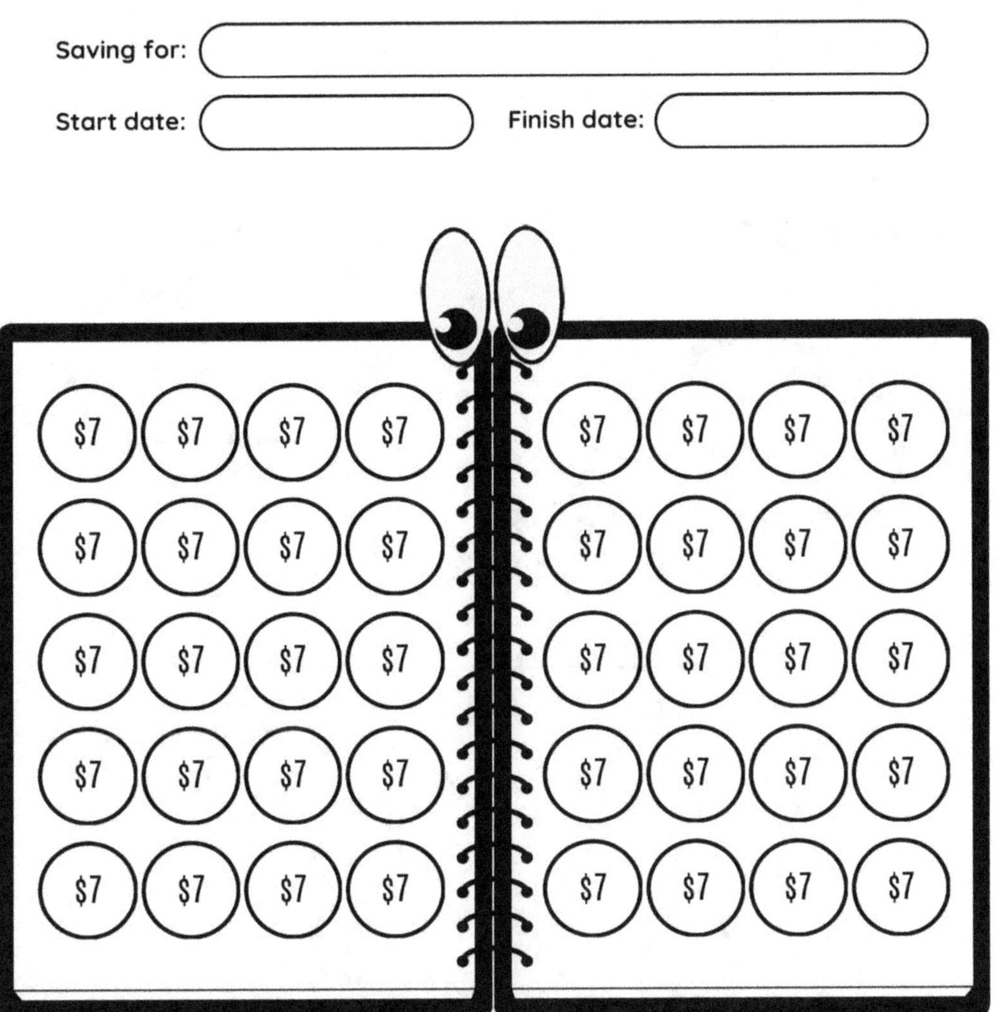

Goal = $280

Saving for:

Start date: Finish date:

Goal = $105

Goal = $100

Goal = $90

Goal = $360

Saving for:

Start date: Finish date:

Goal = $104

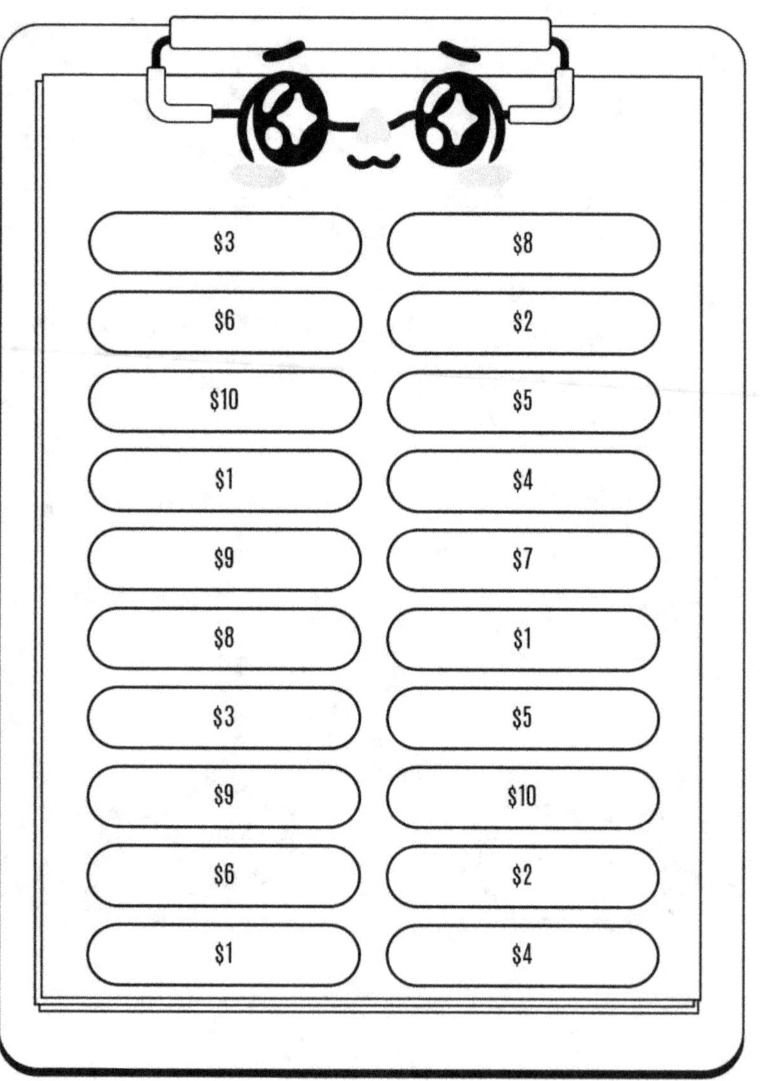

Saving for:

Start date: Finish date:

Each = $3

Goal = $60

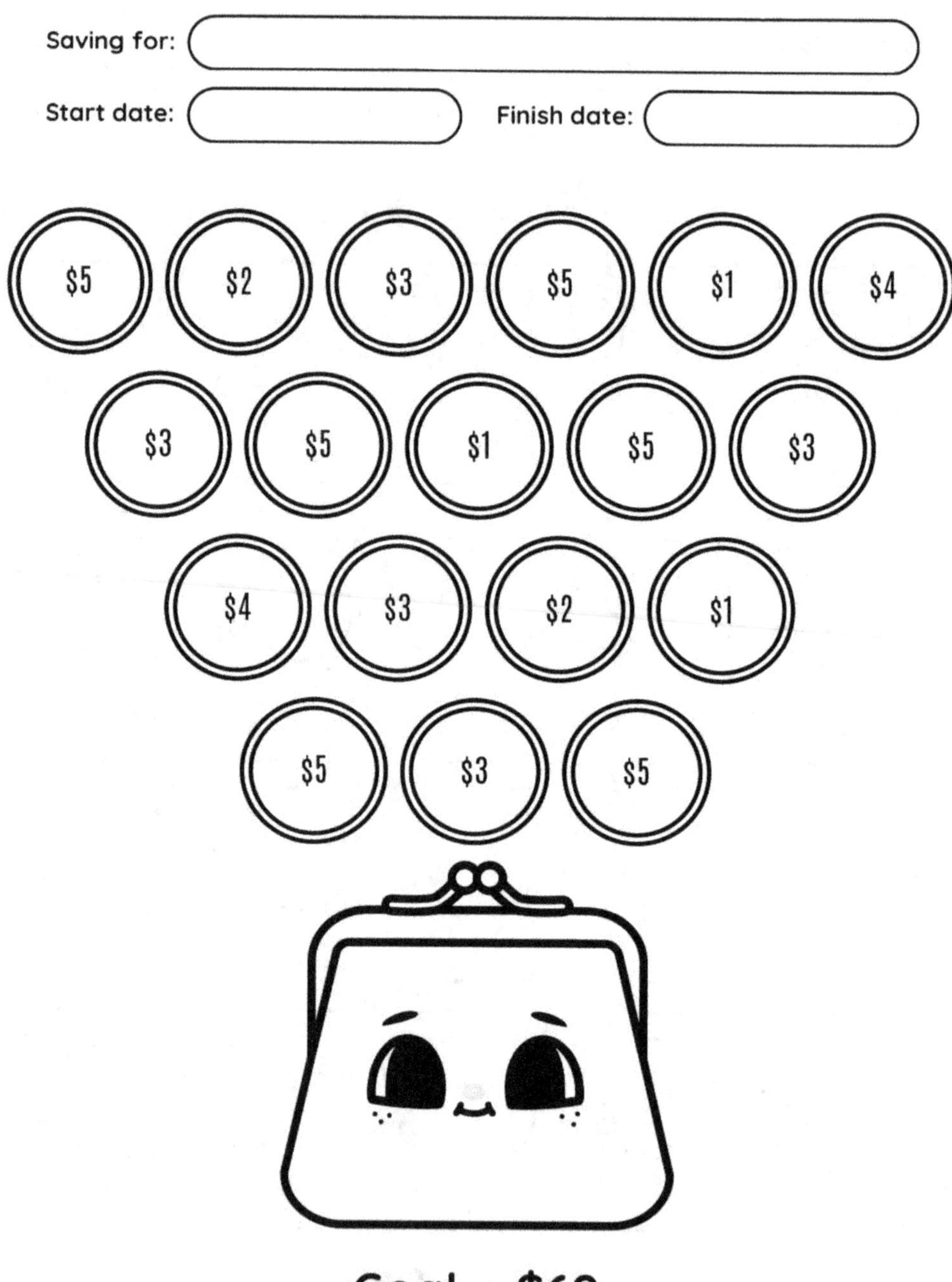

Saving for:
Start date:
Finish date:
$5
$2
$3
$5
$1
$4
$3
$5
$1
$5
$3
$4
$3
$2
$1
$5
$3
$5
Goal = $60

Saving for:

Start date: Finish date:

Goal = $40

Goal = $53

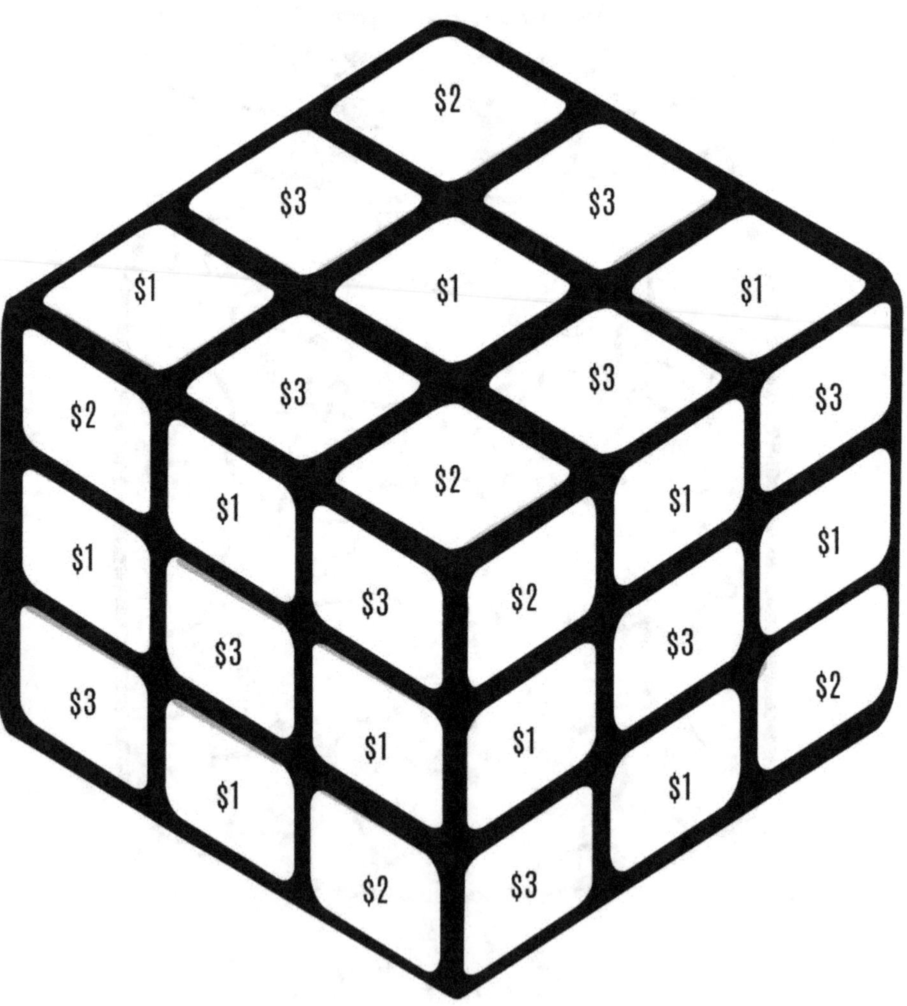

Saving for:

Start date: Finish date:

Goal = $58

Saving for:

Start date: Finish date:

Make Your Own Challenge

Goal:

Saving for:

Start date: Finish date:

Make Your Own Challenge

Goal:

Saving for:

Start date: Finish date:

Make Your Own Challenge

Goal:

Make Your Own Challenge

Saving for:

Start date: Finish date:

Make Your Own Challenge

Goal:

Saving for:

Start date: Finish date:

Make Your Own Challenge   Goal:

30-Day
Savings
Challenges

Duration: 30 Days
Goal: $100
Start Date: _________
Finish Date: _________

START
$1
$2
$3
$4
$5
$1
$3
$5
$2
$5
$3
$4
$2
$4
$1
$3
$1
$4
$3
$2
$4
$5
$3
$2
$5
$4
$4
$5
$4
$2
$5
$3
FINISH

Duration: 30 Days

Goal: $1000

Start Date: __________

Finish Date: __________

Let's begin here!

$5 | $10 | $20 | $30 | $40

$25

$55 | $30 | $45 | $40 | $35 | $55 | $35

$15 | $50 | $5

$45

$30 | $55 | $40 | $20

$20 | $50 | $25 | $35 | $30

$40

$35 | $55 | $25

You did it!!

Duration: 30 Days
Start Date: __________

goal: $100
Finish Date: __________

Fill the
piggy bank

$3
$2
$4
$1
$3
$5
$5
$4
$5
$3
$1
$4
$5
$3
$5
$3
$4
$2
$1
$5
$1
$5
$4
$2
$5
$1
$5
$5
$3
$4
$1
$2
$3
$4
$5

Duration: 30 Days

Goal: $500

Start Date: __________

Finish Date: __________

You did it!

$25
$5
$15
$25
$5
$15
$10
$20
$5
$25
$30
$20
$5
$30
$15
$10
$5
$20
$15
$25
$15
$30
$5
$15
$10
$30
$20
$15

Start Here!

Duration: 30 Days
Start Date: __________
Goal: $500
Finish Date: __________

Great job!
$5 $10 $15 $25
$15 $20 $5 $30
$25 $5 $20 $10 $25
$20 $25 $5 $30 $15
$30 $5 $25 $15 $5 $10
$5 $10 $15 $20 $25 $30
Let's start here...

Duration: 30 Days
Goal: $1000
Start Date: __________
Finish Date: __________
Let's get started!
$5
$10
$20
$30
$40
$25
$35
$55
$35
$40
$45
$30
$55
$15
$50
$5
$45
$30
$55
$40
$20
$30
$35
$35
$40
$20
$50
$25
$55
$25
Congratulations!

Duration: 30 Days
Start Date: _ _ _ _ _ _ _ _ _
Goal: No Spend
Finish Date: _ _ _ _ _ _ _ _ _
Let's start here

Duration: 30 Days
Goal: No Spend
Start Date: __________
Finish Date: __________

You're doing great!
Start from here

Duration: 30 Days
Start Date: __________
Goal: $ _____________
Finish Date: __________

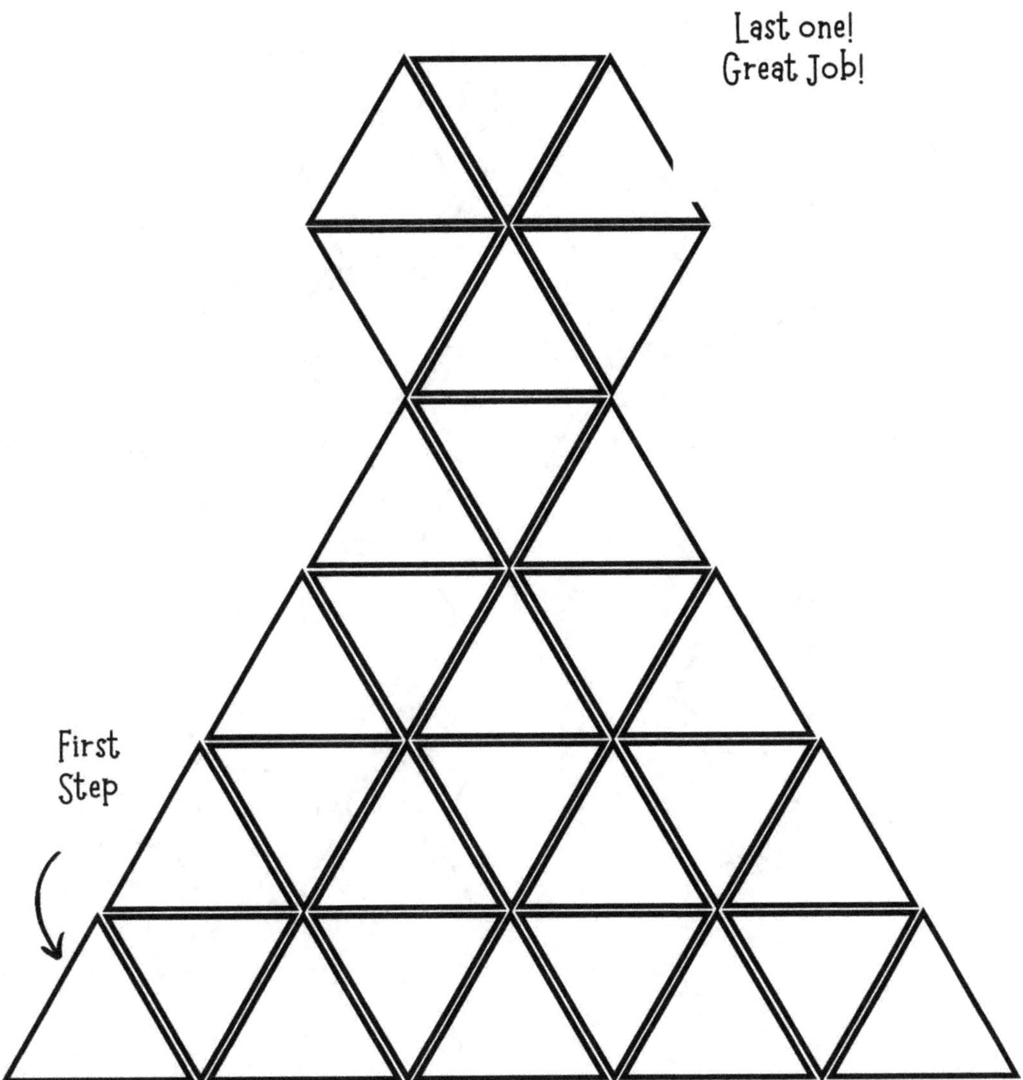

Last one!
Great Job!
First
Step

Duration: 30 Days
Goal: $ ____________
Start Date: __________
Finish Date: __________

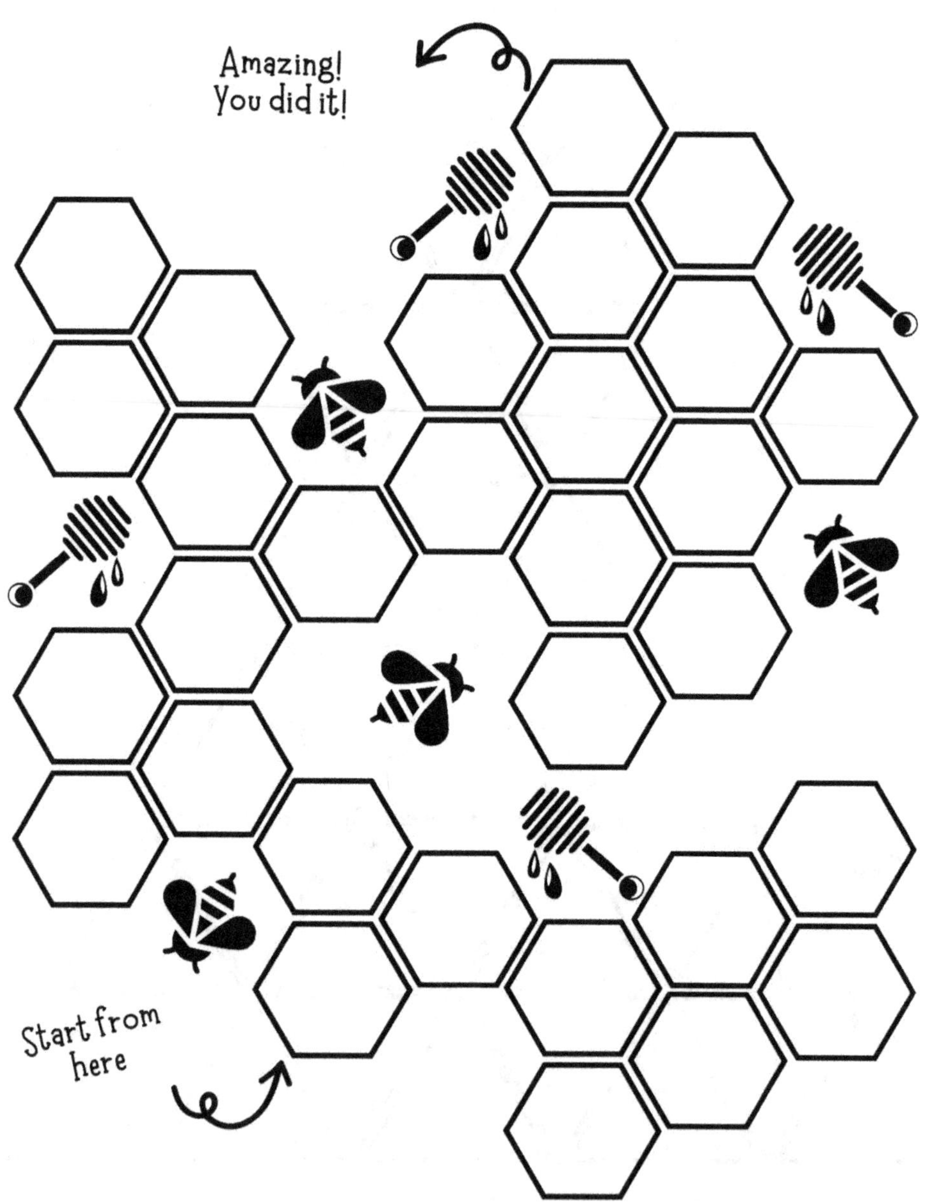
Amazing!
You did it!
Start from
here

Duration: 30 Days

Start Date: __________

Goal: $ ____________

Finish Date: __________

day savings

Start!

challenge

You did great!

Duration: 30 Days

Start Date: __________

Goal: $ _____________

Finish Date: __________

Start!

Finish!!!

50-Day
Savings
Challenges

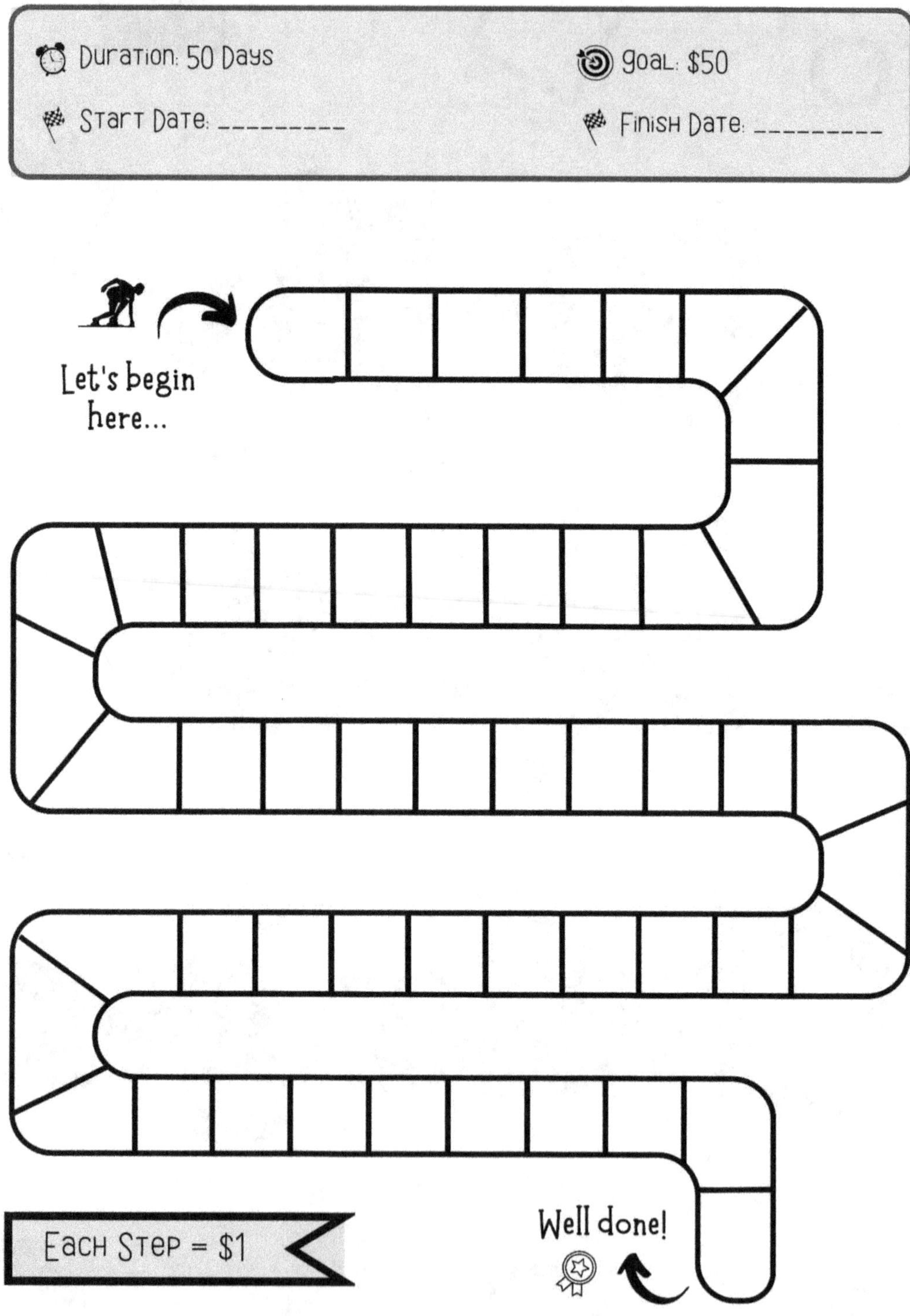

Duration: 50 Days
Start Date: __________
Goal: $50
Finish Date: __________
Let's begin here...
Each Step = $1
Well done!

Each Candy Heart= $1

Duration: 50 Days

Goal: $100

Start Date: __________

Finish Date: __________

AMAZING!
You did it!

START
HERE

Each Tulip = $2

Duration: 50 Days

Goal: $100

Start Date: __________

Finish Date: __________

Duration: 50 Days
Start Date: _________
Goal: $150
Finish Date: __________
Well done!
You did it
You can
start here
Each Star = $3

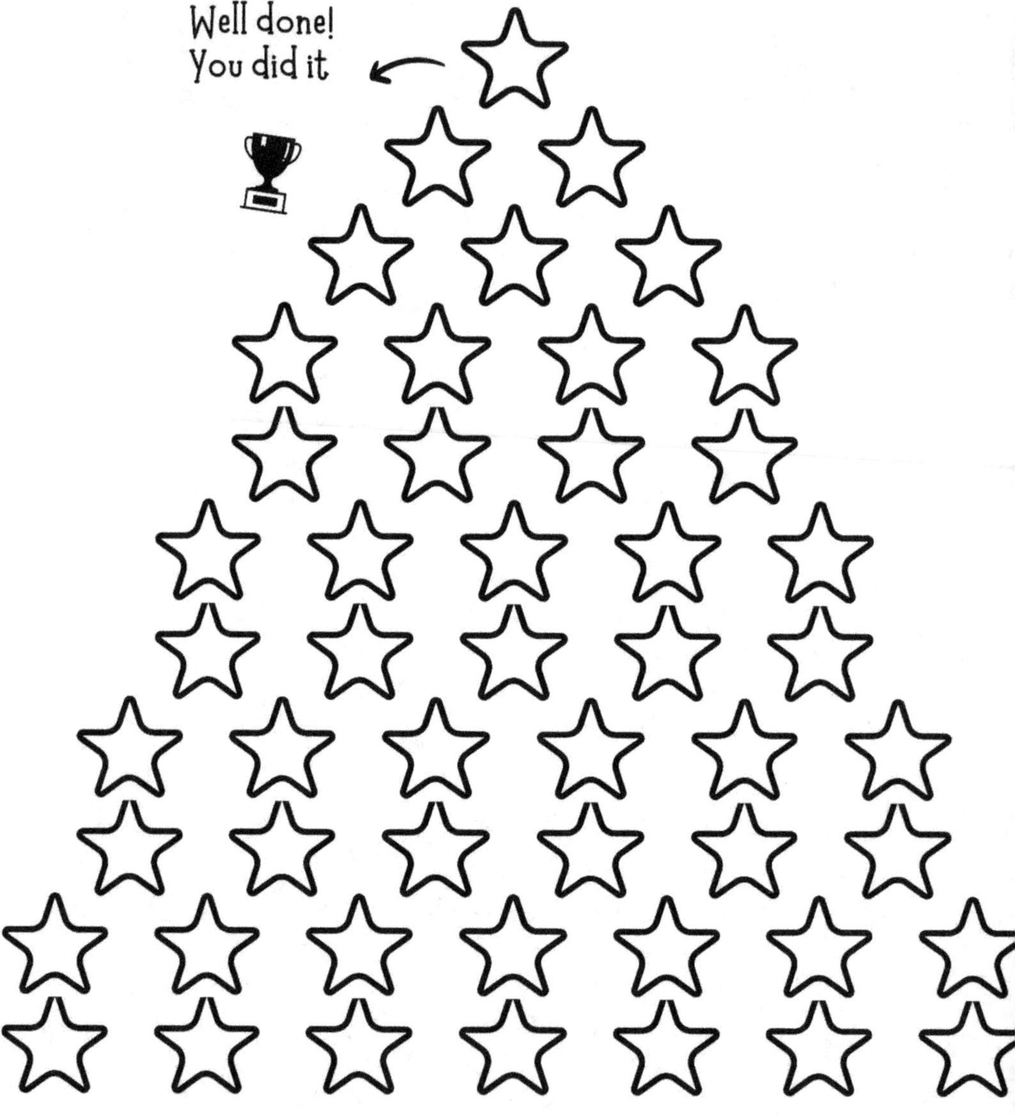

Duration: 50 Days
Goal: $150
Start Date: __________
Finish Date: __________

You did great!

Begin here!
Each Bottle= $3

Duration: 50 Days
Start Date: __________
Goal: $200
Finish Date: __________
You did it!
Start here!
Each Plant = $4

Duration: 50 Days
Start Date: __________
Goal: $200
Finish Date: __________

You've done
it again!

Let's
start
here!

Each Medal= $4

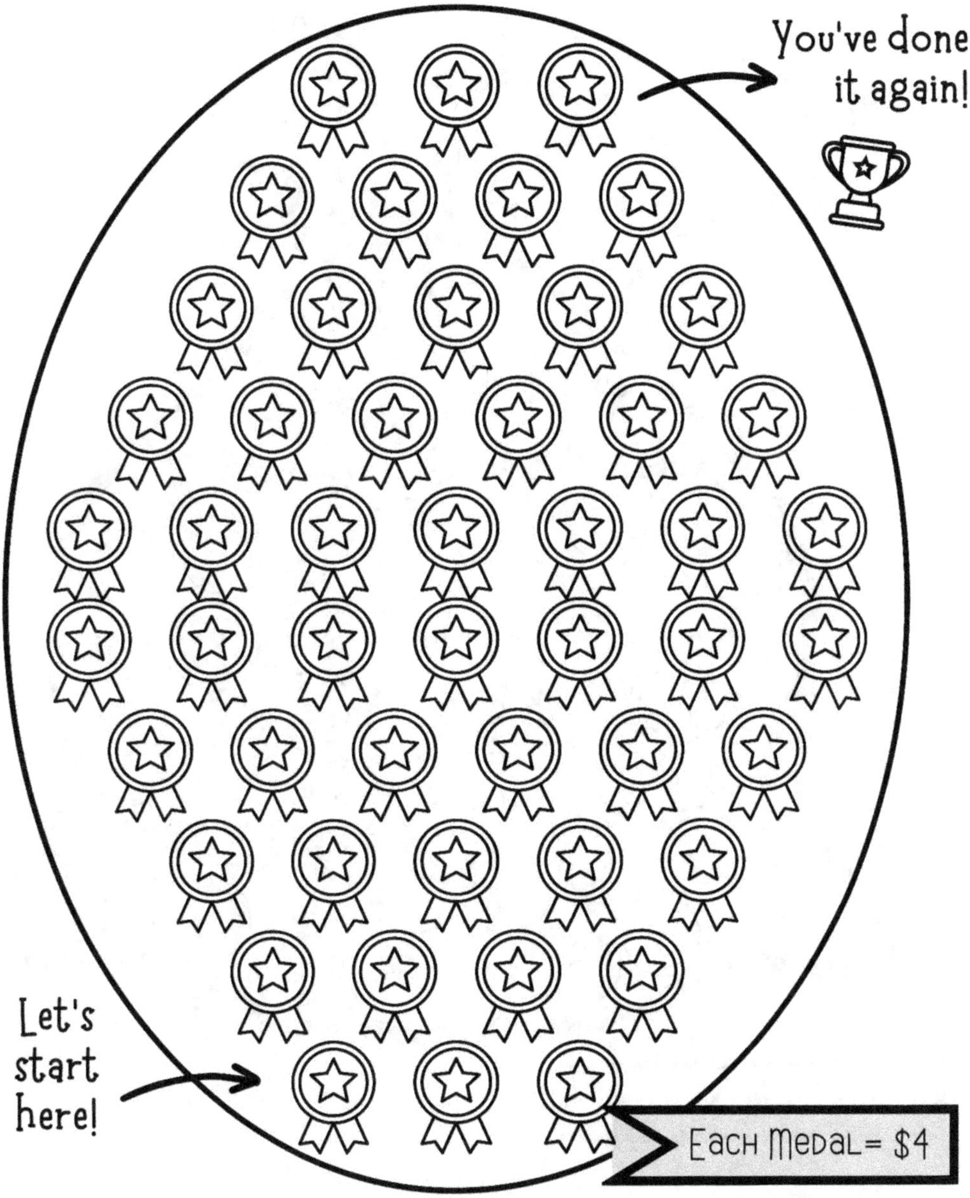

Duration: 50 Days
Start Date: __________
Goal: $250
Finish Date: __________ 
Wow! You did it!
Each Coin = $5
Start Here!

Duration: 50 Days
Start Date: __________
Goal: $250
Finish Date: __________ 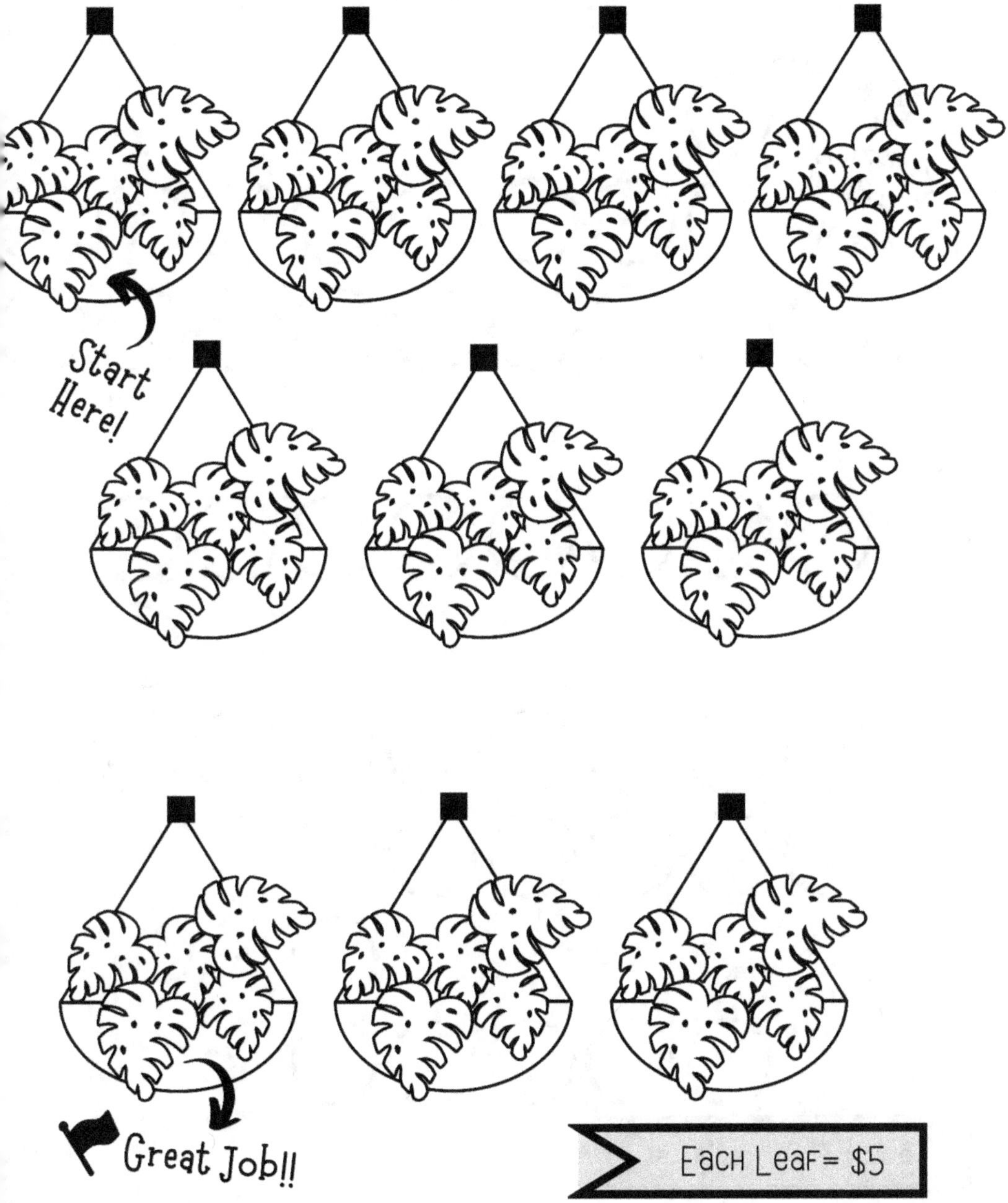
Start Here!
Great Job!!
Each Leaf = $5

Duration: 50 Days
Goal: $500
Start Date: __________
Finish Date: __________
Amazing! You did it again!
$25
Let's begin here!
Each Step = $10

Duration: 50 Days
Start Date: __________
Goal: $500
Finish Date: __________
Great work!
Half way there!
Start here!
Each Step= $10

Duration: 50 Days

Goal: $750

Start Date: __________

Finish Date: __________

Great Job!

Let it

Grow

Start here!

Each Leaf = $15

Duration: 50 Days
Start Date: __________
Goal: $750
Finish Date: __________
Wow! You made it!
Start here!
Each Chat Bubble = $10

Duration: 50 Days
Goal: $1000
Start Date: __________
Finish Date: __________
That's Amazing!
Start here!
Each Cookie = $20

Duration: 50 Days
Goal: $1000
Start Date: __________
Finish Date: __________ 
Great! You did it!
Start here!
Each Cup= $20

Duration: 50 Days
Goal: $1250
Start Date: __________
Finish Date: __________

Each Ornament = $25

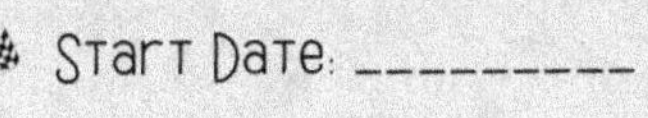 Duration: 50 Days

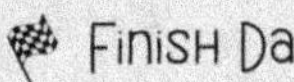 Goal: $1250

🏁 Start Date: __________

🏁 Finish Date: __________

Each Egg = $25

Duration: 52 Weeks
Goal: $2000
Start Date: __________
Finish Date: __________
$50
$40
Super!
You did it!
$50
$55
$40
$35
$45
$30
$10
$50
$45
$40
$25
$35
$30
$50
$50
$35
$45
$20
$30
$20
$25
$50
$25
$40
$25
$30
$30
$55
$50
$25
$40
$50
$25
$40
$30
$40
$25
$50
$40
$35
$45
$50
$25
$50
$40
$50
$40
$50
$35
$65
$40
Start
here!
$40

Duration: 52 Weeks
Goal: $15000
Start Date: __________
Finish Date: __________

Start!

$250 $285 $300 $290 $305
$300 $305 $290 $300 $225 $300 $285
$290 $280 $300 $270 $295 $300 $275
$295 $300 $325 $300 $200 $295 $300
$300 $280 $300 $325 $300 $295 $300
$290 $305 $285 $300 $275 $295 $300
$275 $300 $285 $290 $300 $200 $300

Fantastic! You made it!
$345 $300 $295 $300 $200

Duration: 50 Days

Goal: $1500

Start Date: __________

Finish Date: __________

Well done!

Start!

Each Flower = $30

Duration: 50 Days
Goal: $1500
Start Date: __________
Finish Date: __________
Great Job!
Start!
Each Butterfly = $30

Duration: 50 Days
Start Date: __________
Goal: $2000
Finish Date: __________

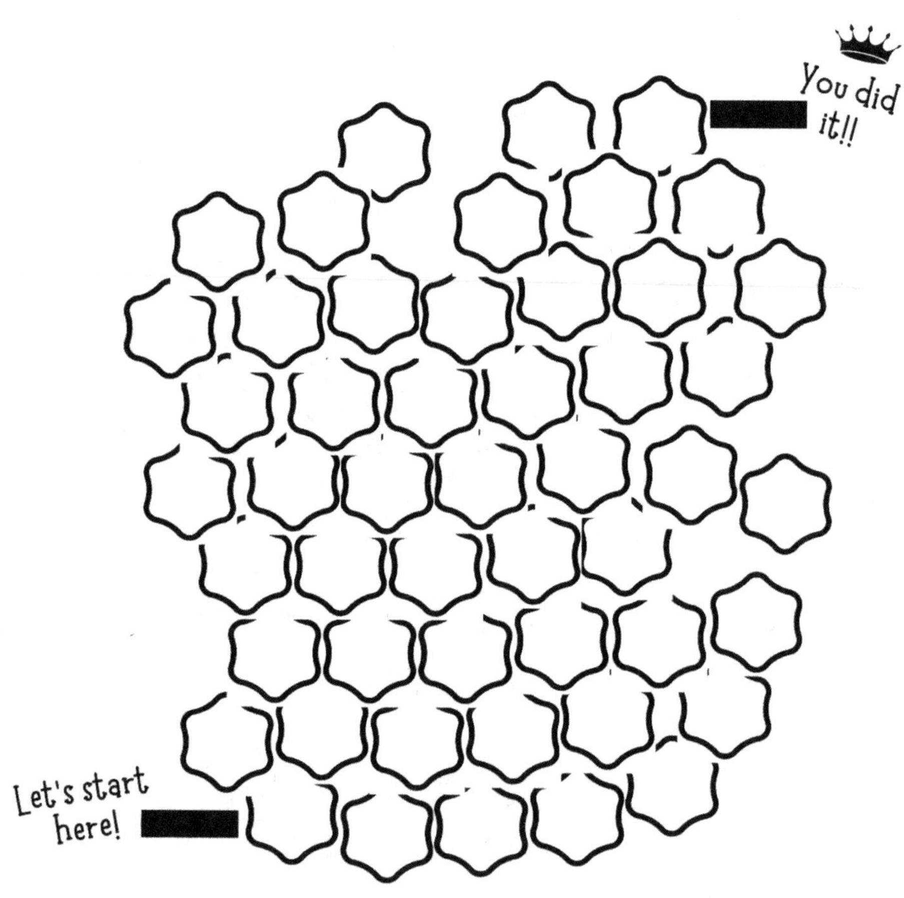

You did it!!
Let's start here!

Each Spot = $40

Duration: 50 Days
Goal: $2000
Start Date: __________
Finish Date: __________
Great Job!
Each Heart= $40
Let's start here!

Duration: 50 Days
Goal: $2500
Start Date: __________
Finish Date: __________
Each Footstep= $50
YOU DID IT!
START

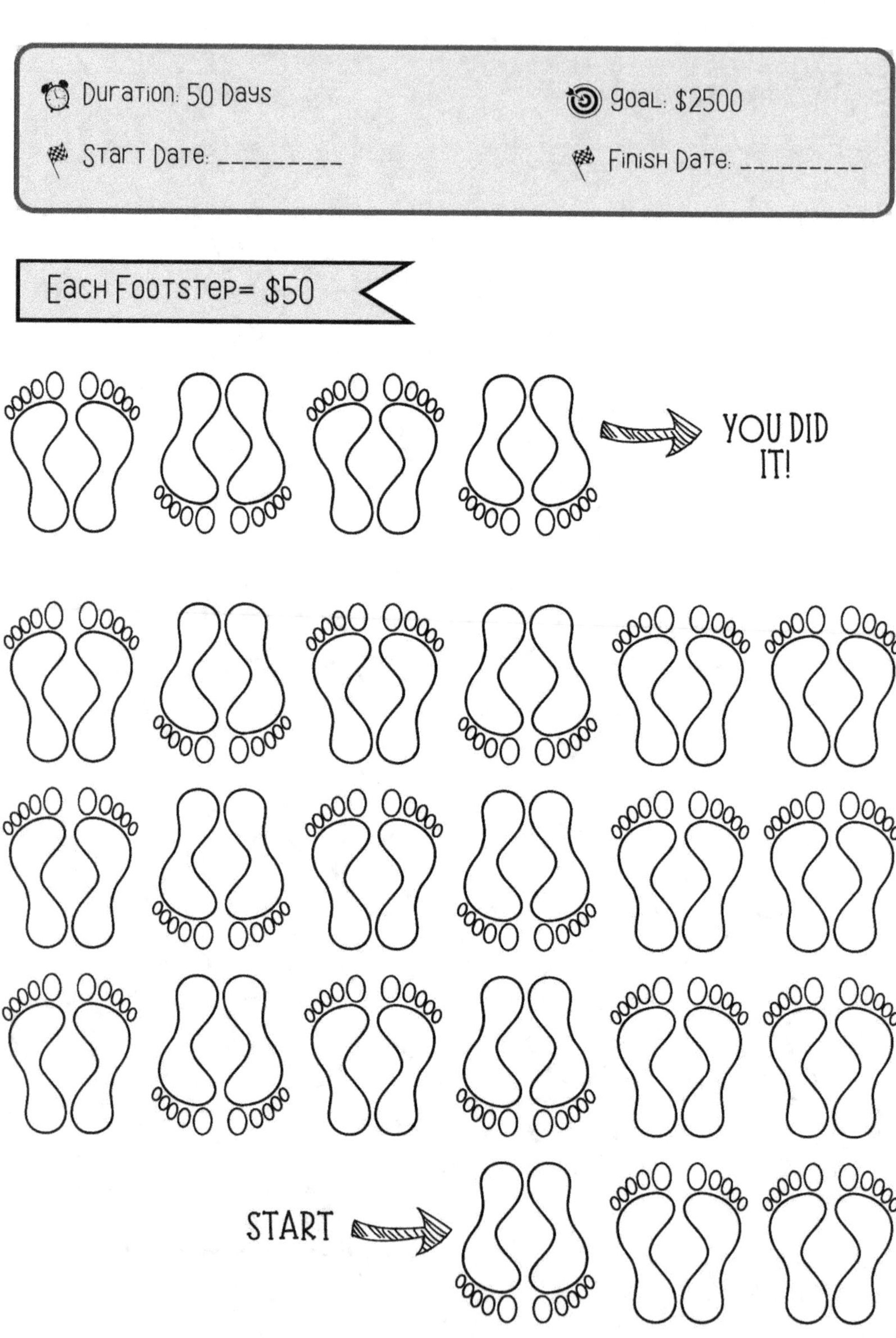

Duration: 50 Days
Start Date: __________
Goal: $2500
Finish Date: __________
Each Droplet = $40
Fill the bucket
Great job!
Start here!

Duration: 50 Days

GoaL: $ ___________

Start Date: __________

Finish Date: __________

Start!

day
savings

challenge

50

You did
great!

Duration: 50 Days
Goal: $ ____________
Start Date: __________
Finish Date: __________
Wonderful!
Let's begin here

⏰ Duration: 50 Days

🎯 Goal: $ _____________

🏁 Start Date: __________

🏁 Finish Date: __________

Good
Job!

Let's
begin
here!

Duration: 50 Days

Goal: $ ____________

Start Date: __________

Finish Date: __________

You
did
it!

Start!

100-Day
Savings
Challenges

Duration: 100 Days
Goal: $500
Start Date: __________
Finish Date: __________

Each Tree= $5

Amazing!
Good Job!

Start here!

Duration: 100 Days

Goal: $500

Start Date: __________

Finish Date: __________

You did it!

Each Honeycomb = $5

Start from here

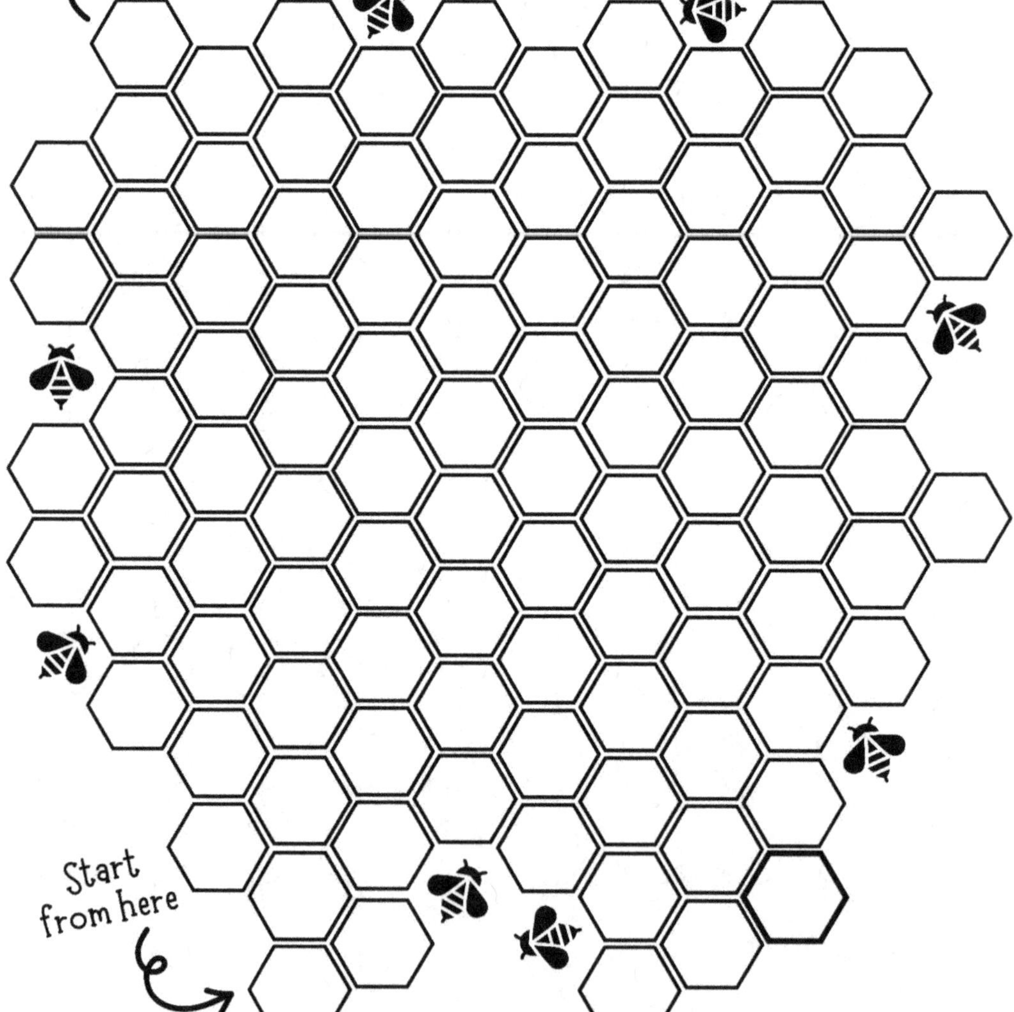

Duration: 100 Days
Goal: $1000
Start Date: __________
Finish Date: __________
Each Box= $10
You made it!
Start here!

Duration: 100 Days
Goal: $1000
Start Date: __________
Finish Date: __________
You did it!
Each Circle= $10
Start here!

Duration: 100 Days
Start Date: __________
Goal: $5000
Finish Date: __________
Each Diamond = $50
Well done!
Start here!

Duration: 100 Days
Goal: $5000
Start Date: __________
Finish Date: __________
Amazing!
Each Circle= $10
Start here!

Duration: 100 Days
Start Date: ___________
Goal: $ _____________
Finish Date: ___________
Great job!
START!

⏰ Duration: 100 Days

🎯 Goal: $ _____________

🏁 Start Date: __________

🏁 Finish Date: __________

Amazing!

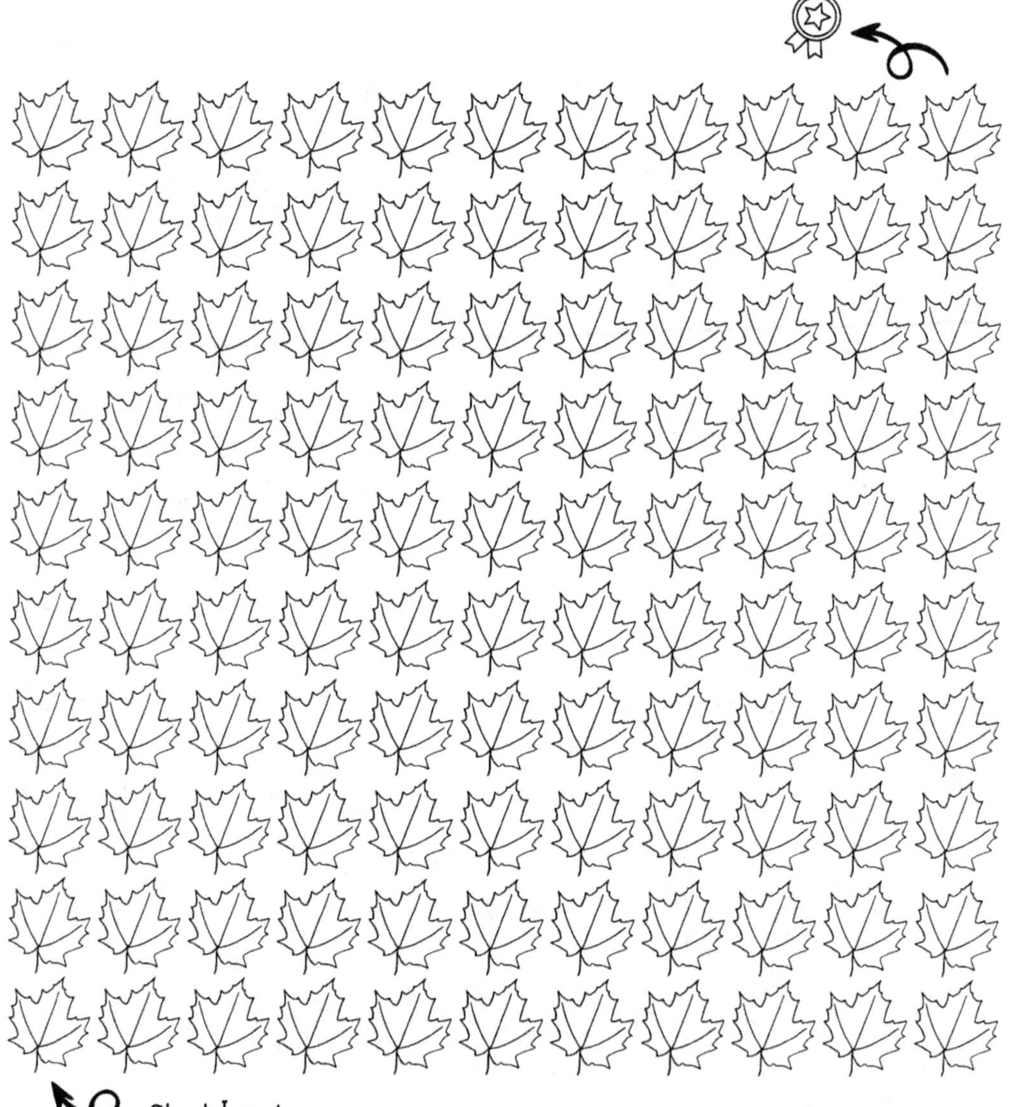

Duration: 100 Days
Goal: $ ____________
Start Date: _________
Finish Date: _________
You did it!
START!

Amazing!

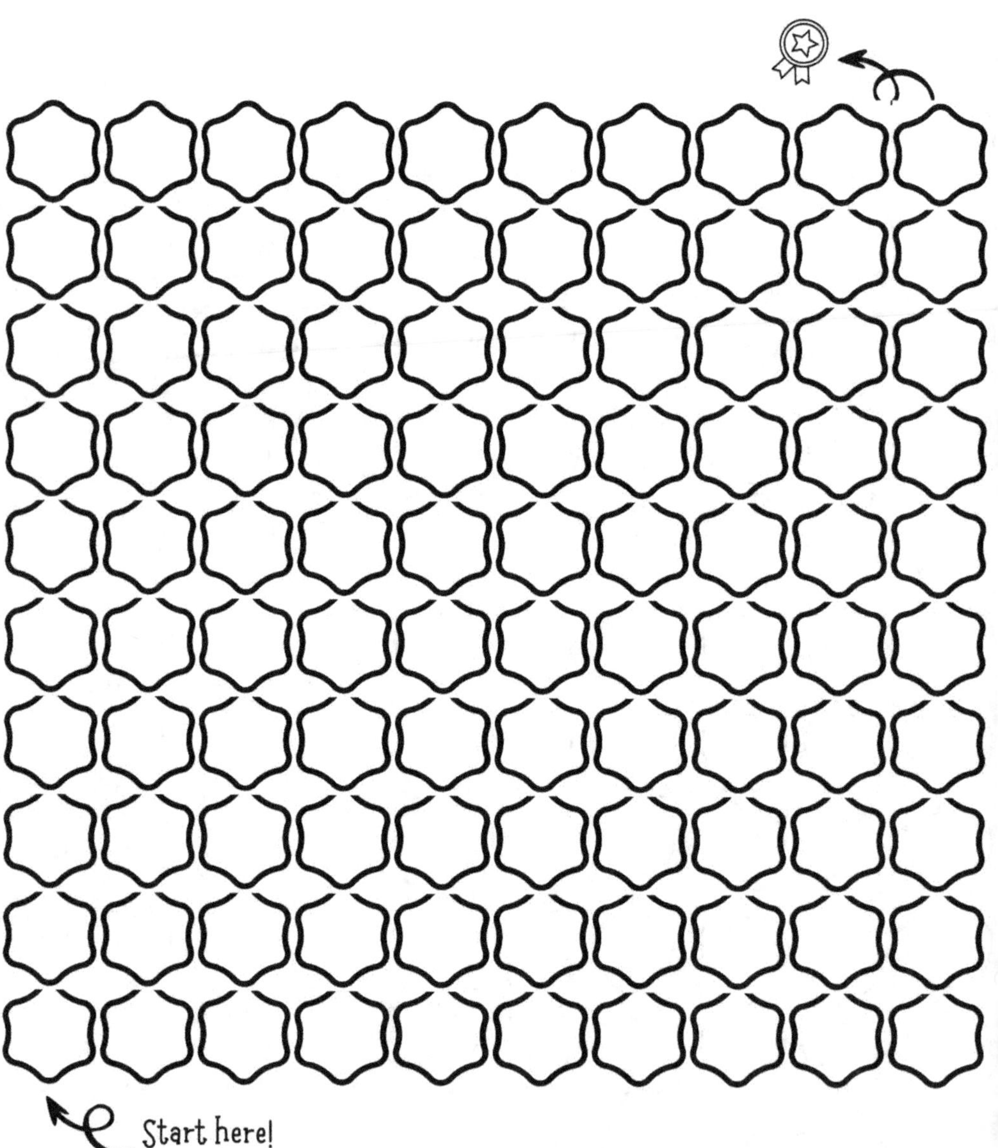

26-Week
Savings
Challenges

Duration: 26 Weeks
Goal: $351
Start Date: __________
Finish Date: __________
Start here!
$1
$2
$3
$4
$5
$6
$7
$8
$9
$10
$11
$12
$13
$14
$15
$16
$17
$18
$19
$20
$21
$22
$23
$24
$25
$26
FORWARD!
Follow the ascending order from $1 to $26
You did it!

Duration: 26 Weeks
Goal: $351
Start Date: __________
Finish Date: __________ 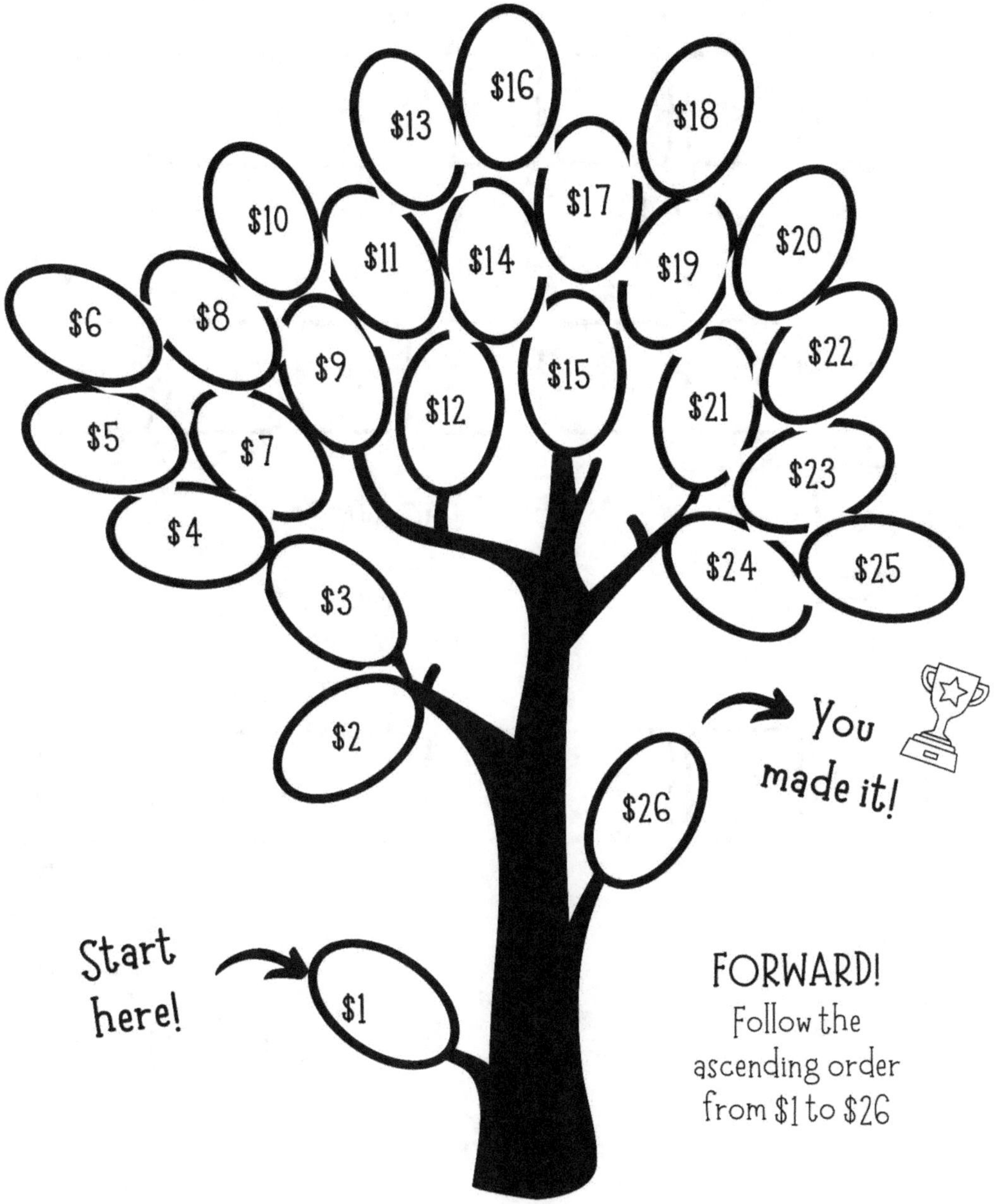
$16
$13
$18
$10
$17
$11
$14
$20
$6
$8
$19
$9
$12
$15
$21
$22
$5
$7
$23
$4
$24
$25
$3
$2
$26
You made it!
$1
Start here!
FORWARD!
Follow the ascending order from $1 to $26

Duration: 26 Weeks
Goal: $351
Start Date: __________
Finish Date: __________

$1
$2
$3
$4
$5
$6
$7
$8
$9
$10
$11
$12
$13
$14
$15
$16
$17
$18
$19
$20
$21
$22
$23
$24
$25
$26

Great Job!

BACKWARD!
Follow the
descending order
from $26 to $1

Start here!

Duration: 26 Weeks
Goal: $351
Start Date: __________
Finish Date: __________
Start here! 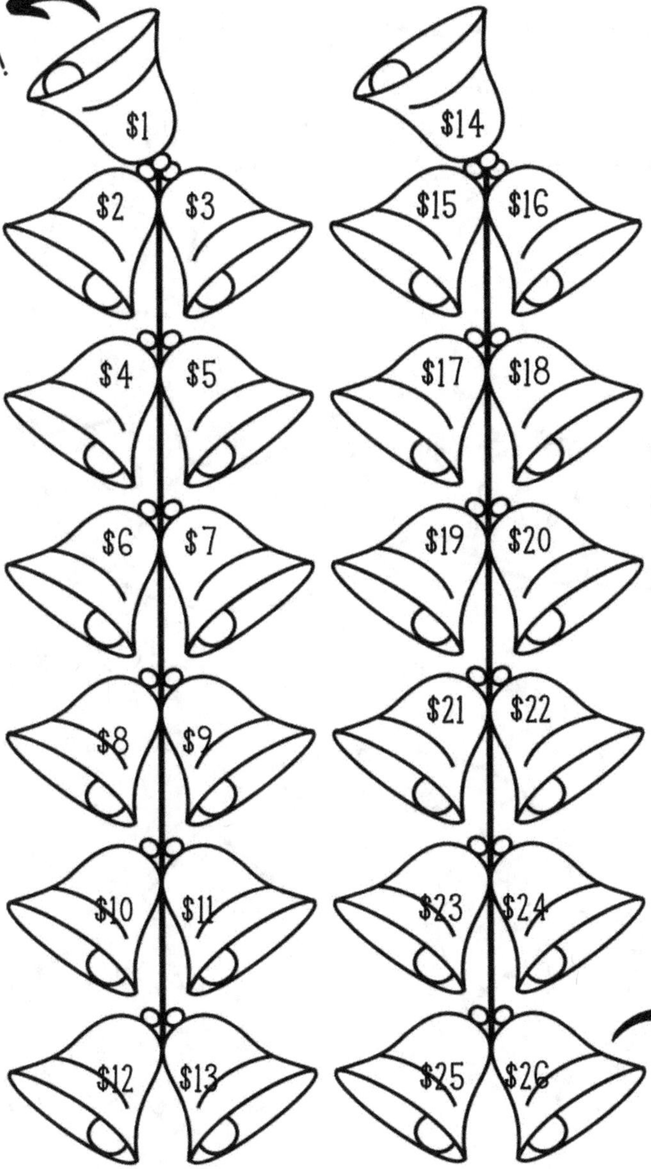
$1
$2
$3
$4
$5
$6
$7
$8
$9
$10
$11
$12
$13
$14
$15
$16
$17
$18
$19
$20
$21
$22
$23
$24
$25
$26
BACKWARD!
Follow the descending order from $26 to $1
Excellent Job!

Duration: 26 Weeks
Start Date: __________
Goal: $702
Finish Date: __________

Start here!

$2
$4
$6
$8
$10
$12
$14
$16
$18
$20
$22
$24
$26
$28
$30
$32
$34
$36
$38
$40
$42
$44
$46
$48
$50
$52

FORWARD!
Follow the
ascending order
from $2 to $52

You did it!

Duration: 26 Weeks
Goal: $702
Start Date: __________
Finish Date: __________

Start here!

$2

FORWARD!
Follow the
ascending order
from $2 to $52

$4 $6 $8

$10 $12 $14 $16

$18 $20 $22 $24 $26

$28 $30 $32 $34 $36 $38

$40 $42 $44 $46 $48 $50 $52

Wonderful!

Duration: 26 Weeks

Goal: $702

Start Date: __________

Finish Date: __________

$44

$42

$40

$8

$6

$46

$38

$10

$4

$48

$36

$12

$2

$50

$34

$14

You made it!

$52

$32

$16

Start!

$30

$18

REVERSE!
Follow the descending order
from $52 to $2

$28

$20

$26

$24

$22

Duration: 26 Weeks

Goal: $702

Start Date: __________

Finish Date: __________

$18

$16

$14

Awesome work!

$12

$2

$20

$22

$6

$4

$24

$26

$10

$8

$30

$36

$42

$44

$28

$32

$46

$48

$34

$40

$38

$52

$50

REVERSE!
Follow the descending order from $52 to $2

Start!

Duration: 26 Weeks
Goal: $2000
Start Date: __________
Finish Date: __________
Start!
Well done!
$65
$85
$70
$50
$75
$75
$80
$65
$100
$50
$60
$50
$90
$90
$75
$75
$100
$80
$100
$80
$55
$100
$75
$95
$70
$90

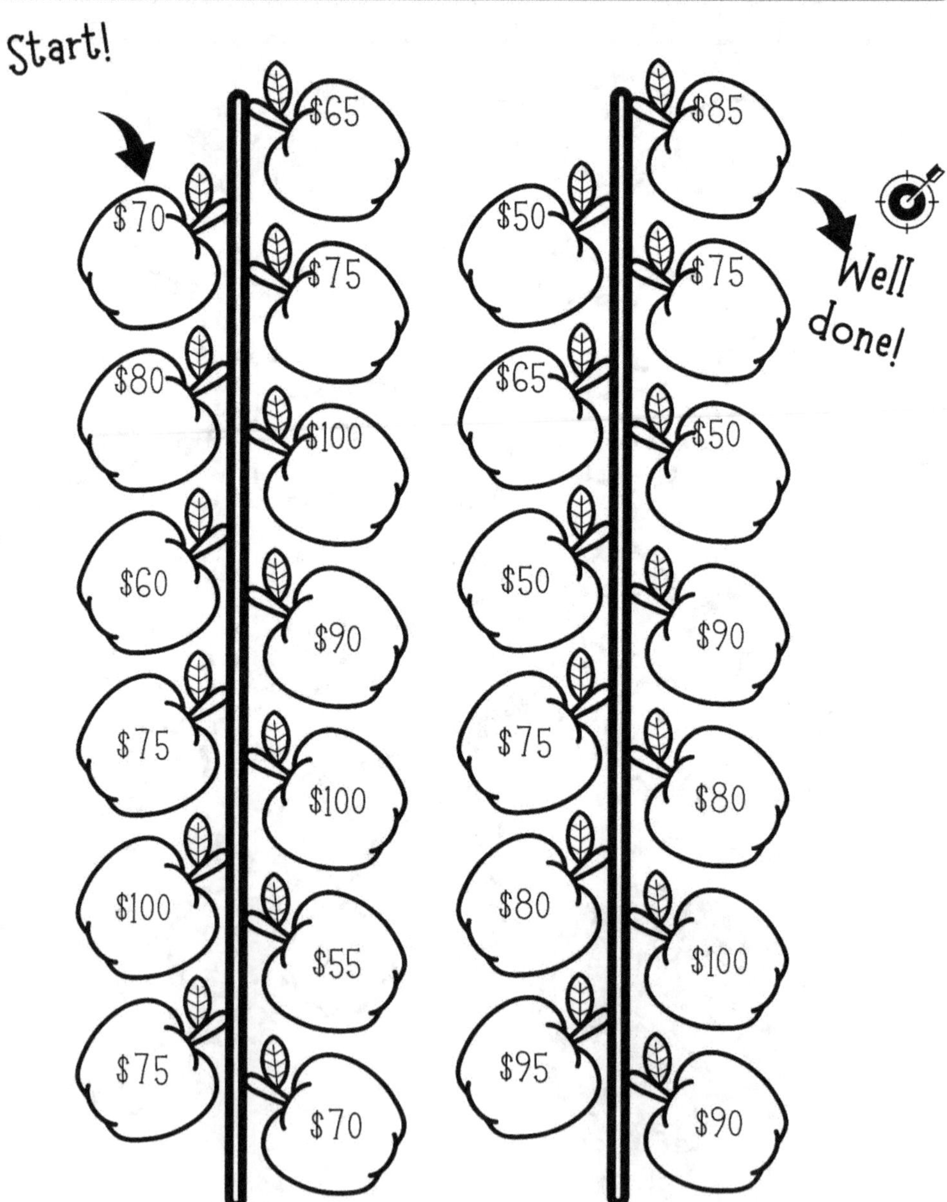

Duration: 26 Weeks
Start Date: __________
Goal: $2000
Finish Date: __________
Start!
$70
$80
$80
$95
$60
$90
$75
$100
$75
$80
$100
$90
$70
$50
You did it!
$55
$75
$100
$75
$90
$85
$100
$75
$65
$50
$50
$65

Duration: 26 Weeks
Goal: $2500
Start Date: __________
Finish Date: __________

$70
$140
$75
$60
$130
You did it!
$100
$120
$80
$90
$150
$100
$80
$70
$90
$70
$105
$120
$85
$100
$90
$100
$90
$100
$90
$75
$120
Start!

Duration: 26 Weeks

Goal: $2500

Start Date: __________

Finish Date: __________

Start here!

$75

$90

$100

$120

$120

$85

$90

$100

$100

$70

$90

$90

$105

$100

$75

$130

$70

$140

$60

$120

$80

$90

$150

$70

$80

$100

You've done it again!

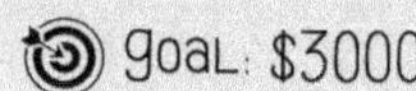

Let's begin here!

$100 $150 $125

$110 $115 $95 $130 $75

$50 $125 $160 $150 $125

$90 $140 $95 $110 $125

$150 $140 $85 $120 $110

$95 $85 $145   Well done!

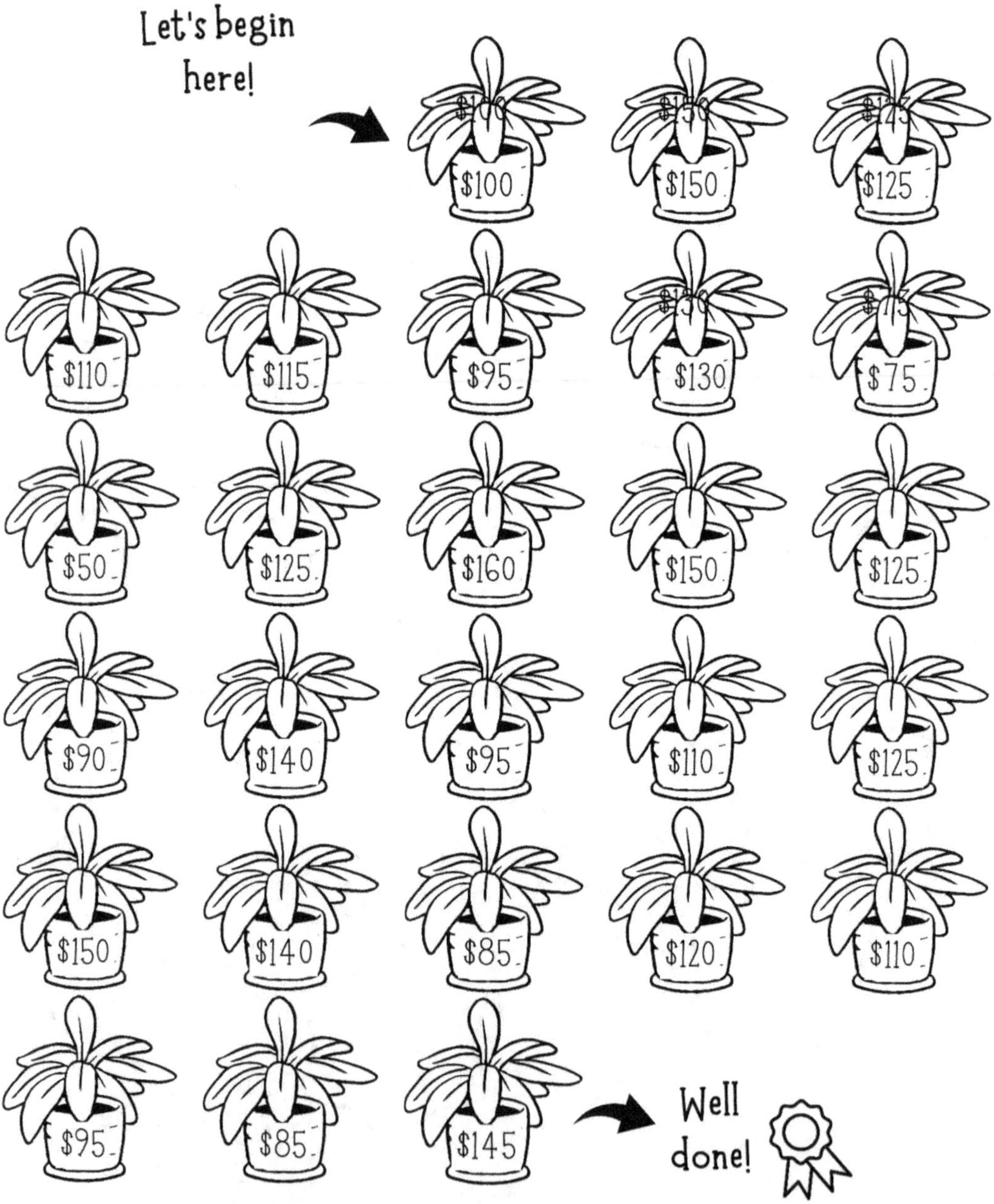

Duration: 26 Weeks

Start Date: _________

Goal: $3000

Finish Date: _________

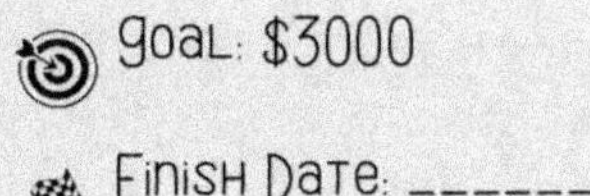

Let's begin here!

		$85	$95	$150
$110	$140	$120	$125	$50
$95	$125	$130	$75	$110
$115	$95	$110	$140	$125
$145	$100	$125	$150	$90
$150	$85	$160		

You did great!

Duration: 26 Weeks
Start Date: __________
Goal: $5000
Finish Date: __________
Amazing!
$250
$110
$300
$175
$120
$200
$275
$225
$250
$120
$275
$250
$250
$60
$150
$225
$200
$275
$200
$150
$325
$120
$175
$75
$125
$90
$100
$300
Start here!

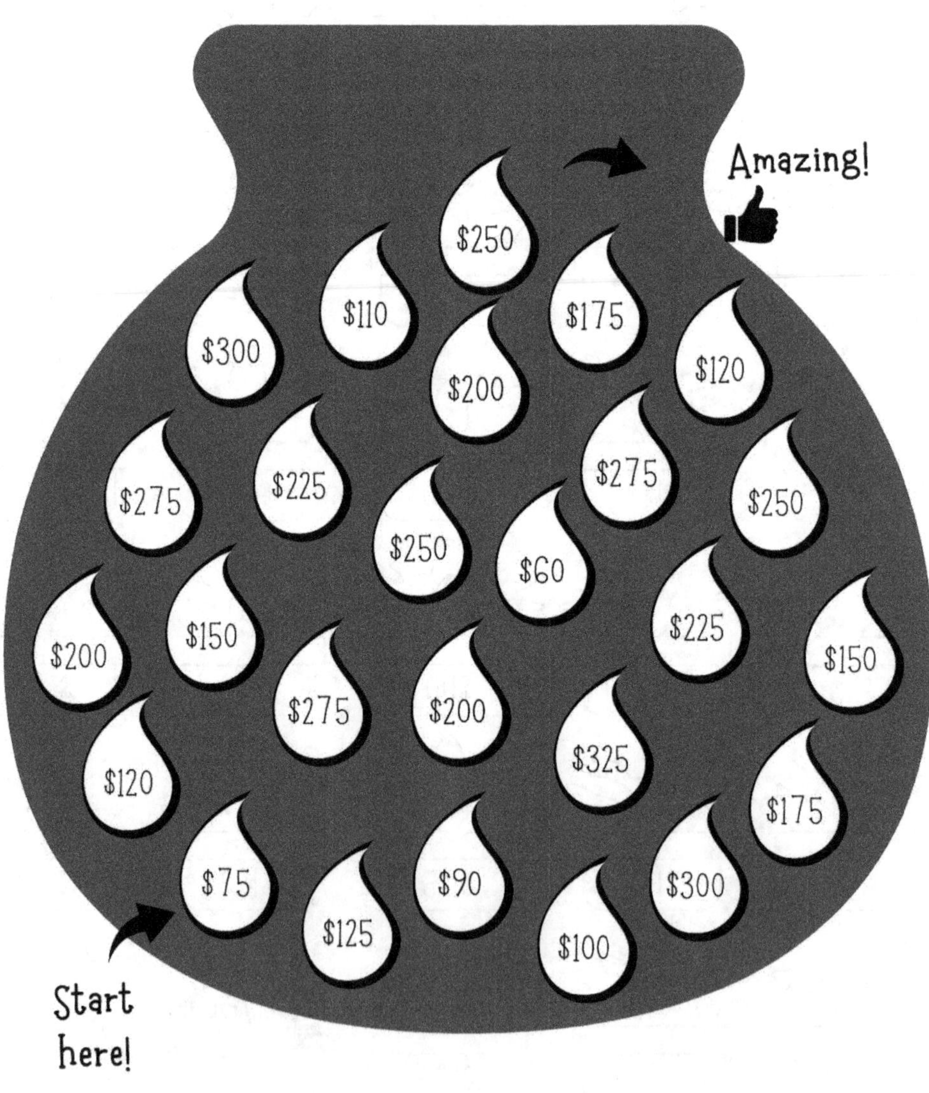

Duration: 26 Weeks
Goal: $5000
Start Date: __________
Finish Date: __________

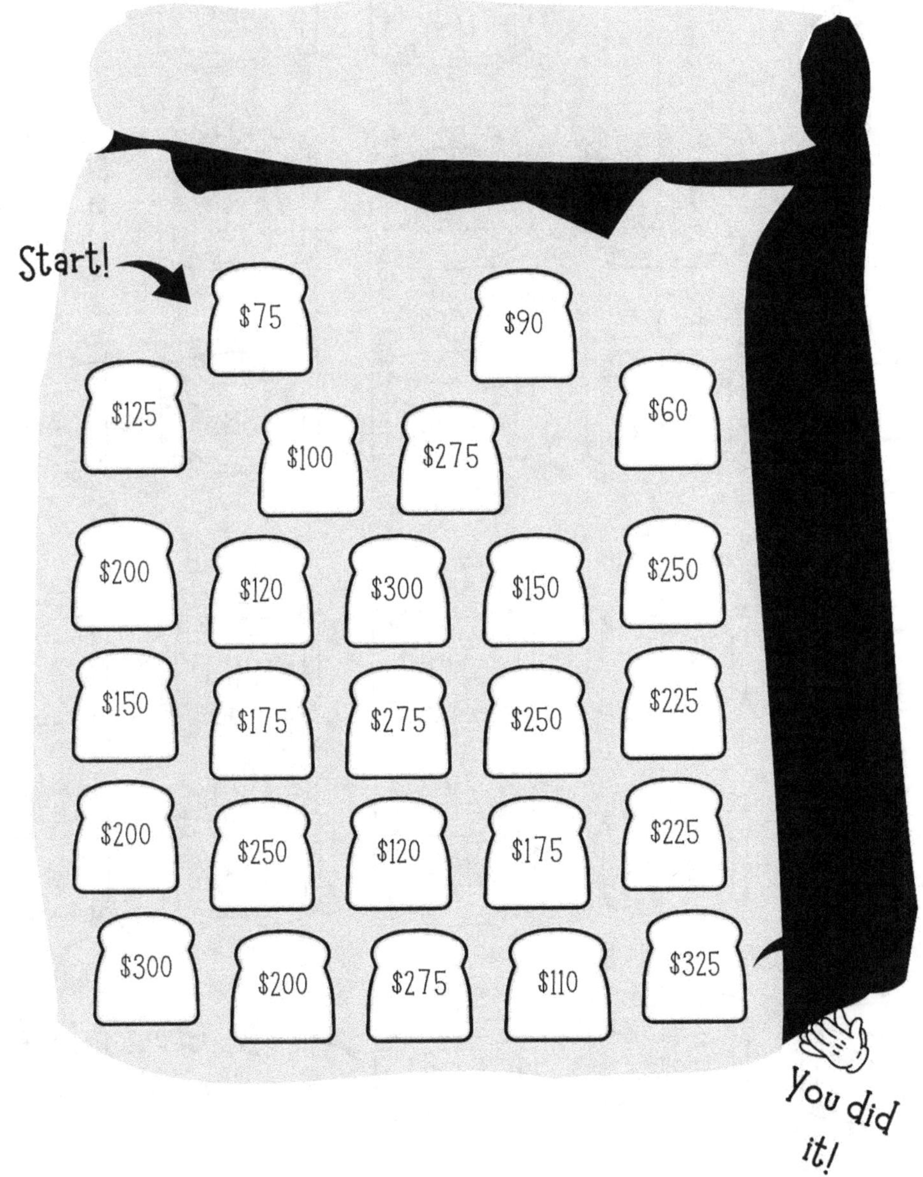

Start!
$75
$90
$125
$60
$100
$275
$200
$120
$300
$150
$250
$150
$175
$275
$250
$225
$200
$250
$120
$175
$225
$300
$200
$275
$110
$325
You did it!

Duration: 26 Weeks
Goal: $10000
Start Date: __________
Finish Date: __________
Start!
$290
$340
$365
$415
$365
$340
$415
$390
$410
$365
$390
$385
$415
$385
$410
$360
$385
$435
$385
$410
$385
$435
$410
$340
$365
$410
Great job!
You did great!

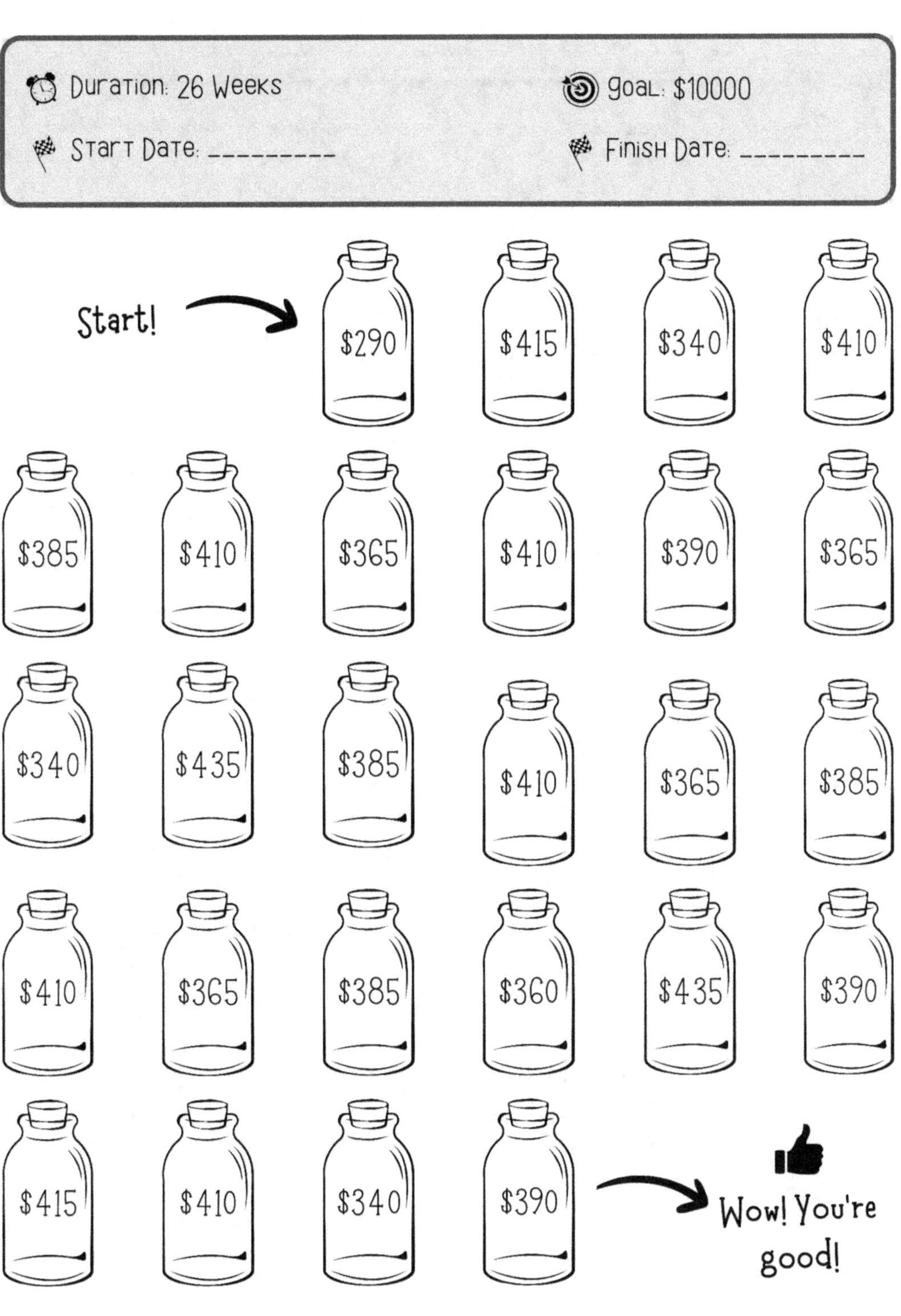

Duration: 26 Weeks
Goal: $10000
Start Date: __________
Finish Date: __________
Start!
$290
$415
$340
$410
$385
$410
$365
$410
$390
$365
$340
$435
$385
$410
$365
$385
$410
$365
$385
$360
$435
$390
$415
$410
$340
$390
Wow! You're good!

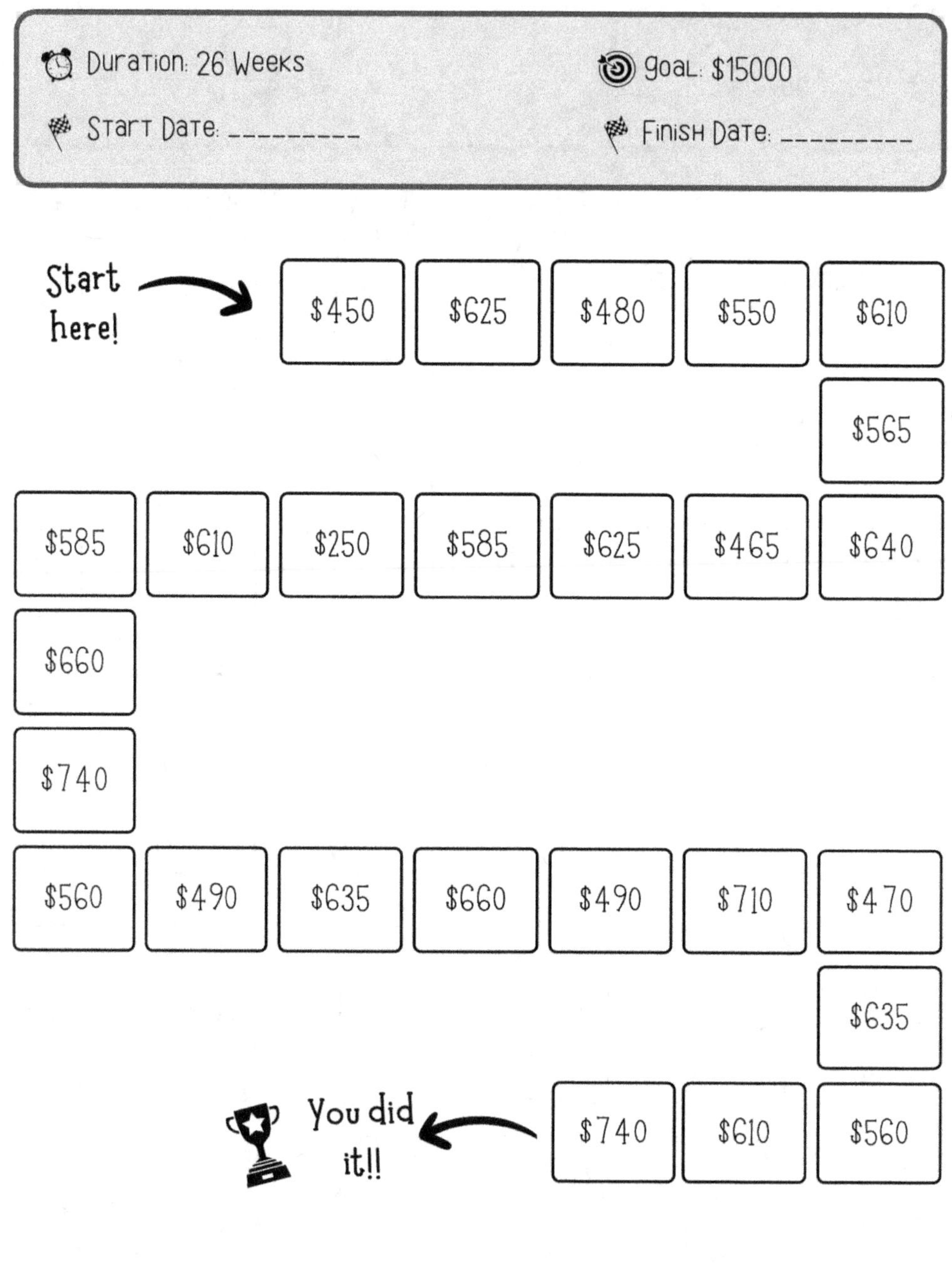

Duration: 26 Weeks
Start Date: __________
Goal: $15000
Finish Date: __________
Start here!
$450
$625
$480
$550
$610
$565
$585
$610
$250
$585
$625
$465
$640
$660
$740
$560
$490
$635
$660
$490
$710
$470
$635
You did it!!
$740
$610
$560

$740	$250
$610	$490
$585	$660
$635	$635
$560	$585
$660	$560
$710	$610
$490	$470
$625	$565
$465	$640
$550	$480
$610	$625
$450	$740

Start anywhere you like...

⏰ Duration: 100 Days
🏁 Start Date: __________
🎯 Goal: $ ____________
🏁 Finish Date: __________

Good Job!
Start here!

Duration: 100 Days

Goal: $ ___________

Start Date: __________

Finish Date: __________

Start here!

Amazing!

Duration: 100 Days
Start Date: __________
Goal: $ _____________
Finish Date: __________

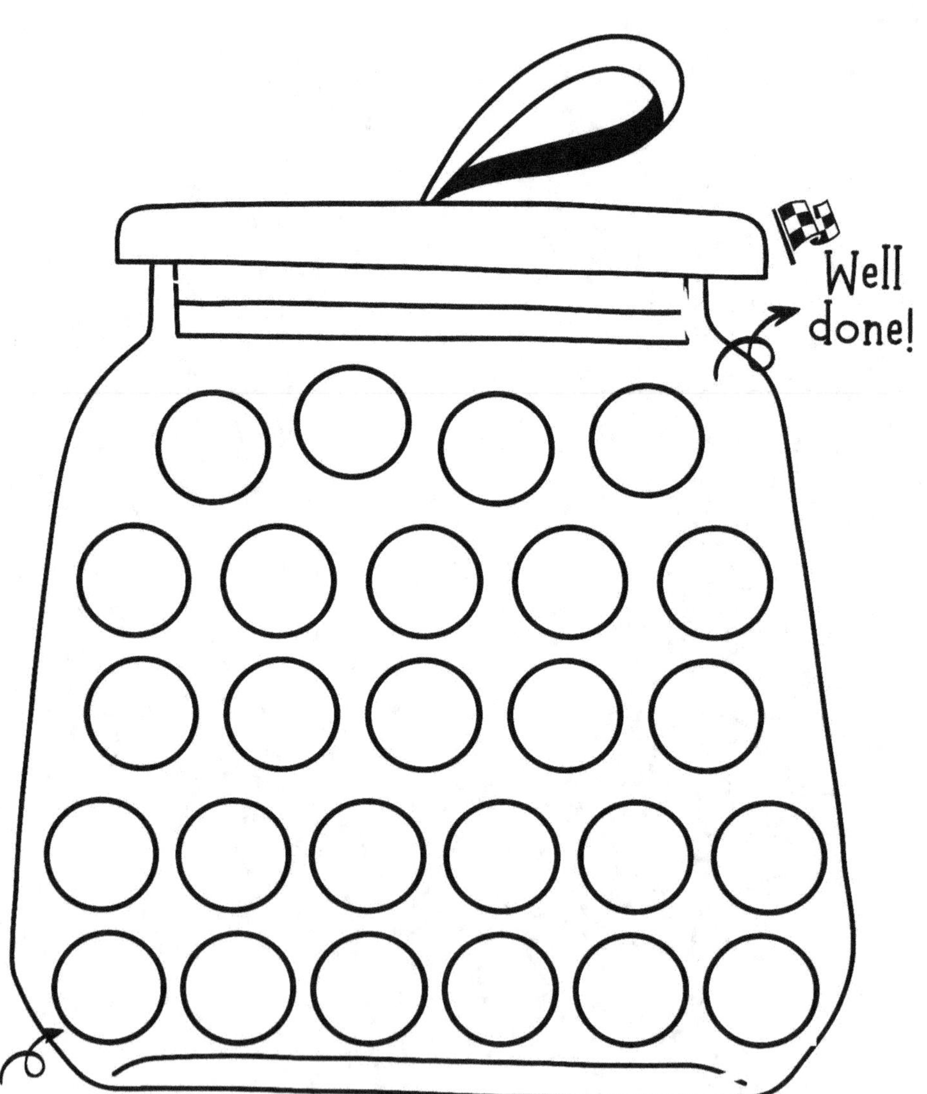

Well done!
Start here!

Duration: 100 Days
Goal: $ ____________
Start Date: __________
Finish Date: __________
You did it!!
Start here!

52-Week
Savings
Challenges

Duration: 52 Weeks
Goal: $1378
Start Date: ___________
Finish Date: ___________

$9
$10
$11
$33
$34
$35
You made it!
$8
$12
$32
$36
$52
$7
$13
$31
$37
$51
$6
$14
$30
$38
$50
$5
$15
$29
$39
$49
$4
$16
$28
$40
$48
$3
$17
$27
$41
$47
$2
$18
$26
$42
$46
$1
$19
$25
$43
$44
$45
$20
$24
Start here!
$21
$22
$23
FORWARD!
Follow the ascending order from $1 to $52

Duration: 52 Weeks

Goal: $1378

Start Date: __________

Finish Date: __________

$9
$10
$11
$33
$34
$35
You made it!

$8
$12
$32
$36
$52

$7
$13
$31
$37
$51

$6
$14
$30
$38
$50

$5
$15
$29
$39
$49

$4
$16
$28
$40
$48

$3
$17
$27
$41
$47

$2
$18
$26
$42
$46

$1
$19
$25
$43
$44
$45

$20
$24

Start here!

$21
$22
$23

FORWARD!
Follow the ascending order from $1 to $52

Duration: 52 Weeks
Goal: $1378 Finish
Start Date: __________
Date: __________

BACKWARD!
Follow the descending order from $52 to $1

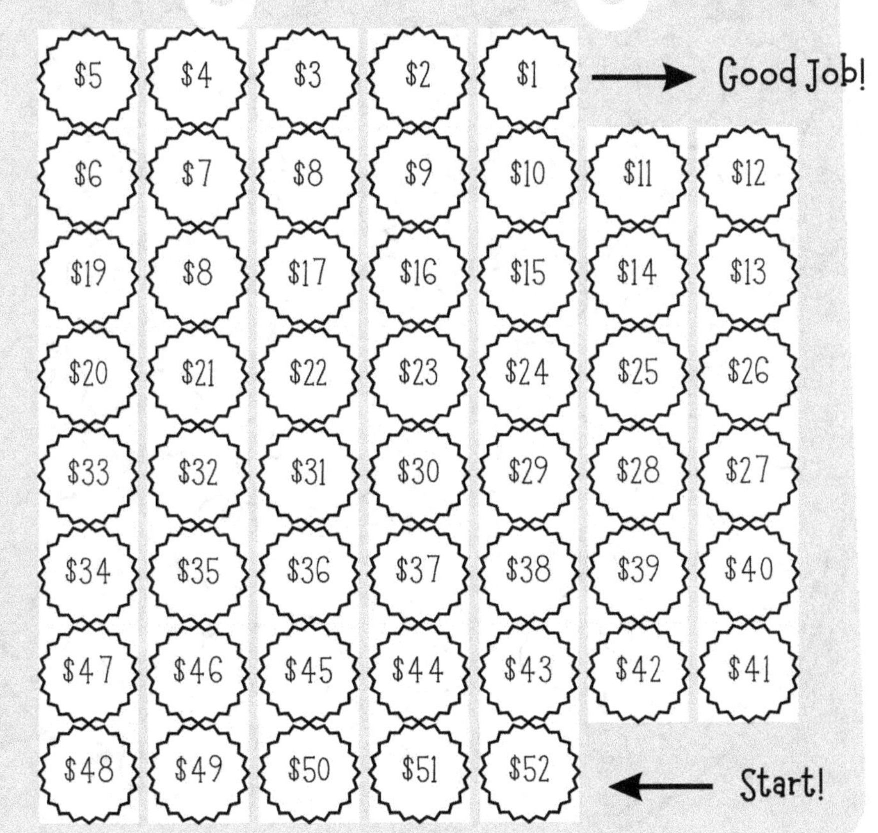
$5 $4 $3 $2 $1 → Good Job!
$6 $7 $8 $9 $10 $11 $12
$19 $8 $17 $16 $15 $14 $13
$20 $21 $22 $23 $24 $25 $26
$33 $32 $31 $30 $29 $28 $27
$34 $35 $36 $37 $38 $39 $40
$47 $46 $45 $44 $43 $42 $41
$48 $49 $50 $51 $52 ← Start!

Duration: 52 Weeks
Start Date: __________
Goal: $1378
Finish Date: __________
BACKWARD!
Follow the descending order from $52 to $1
☆
You did it!!
$3
$2
$1
$4
$5
$6
$7
$12
$11
$10
$9
$8
$14
$13
$20
$21
$16
$17
$18
$19
$15
$23
$22
$28
$27
$26
$25
$24
$35
$29
$30
$31
$32
$33
$34
$36
$42
$41
$40
$39
$38
$37
$48
$43
$44
$45
$46
$47
$52
$49
$50
$51
Start!

Duration: 52 Weeks
Goal: $2756
Start Date: __________
Finish Date: __________ 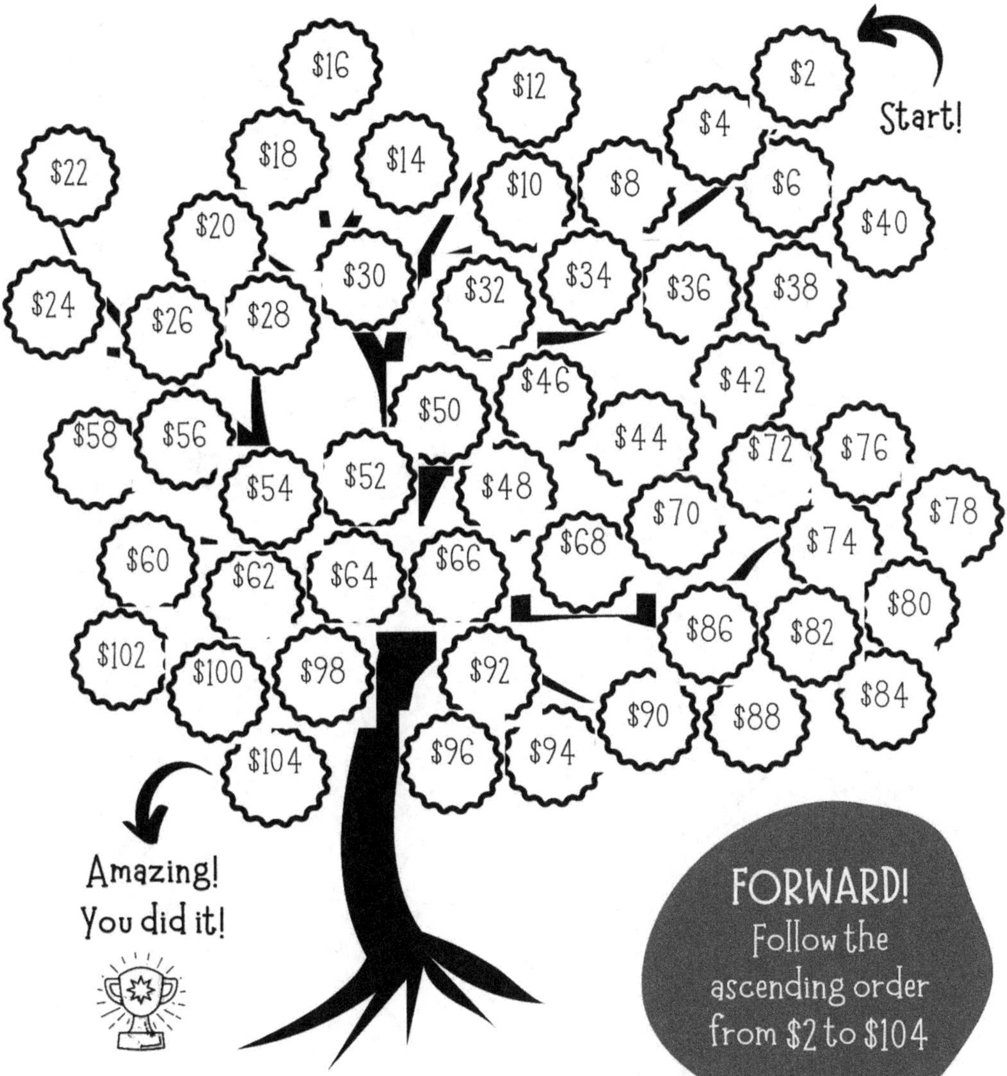
Start!
$2
$4
$6
$40
$12
$8
$10
$16
$14
$18
$34
$36
$38
$22
$20
$30
$32
$42
$24
$26
$28
$46
$44
$72
$76
$58
$56
$50
$48
$70
$74
$78
$54
$52
$68
$80
$60
$62
$64
$66
$86
$82
$102
$100
$98
$92
$90
$88
$84
$104
$96
$94
Amazing!
You did it!
FORWARD!
Follow the
ascending order
from $2 to $104

⏰ Duration: 52 Weeks
🎯 Goal: $2756
🏁 Start Date: __________
🏁 Finish Date: __________

$96
$98
$100
$102
$104
Well done!

$94
$92
$90
$88
$86
$84

$72
$74
$76
$78
80
$82

$70
$68
$66
$64
$62
$60

$48
$50
$52
$54
$56
$58

$46
$44
$42
$40
$38
$36

$24
$26
$28
$30
$32
$34

$22
$20
$18
$16
$14
$12

Start!
$2
$4
$6
$8
$10

Duration: 52 Weeks
Goal: $2756
Start Date: __________
Finish Date: __________
Well done! You did it!
$2
$4
$6
$8
$10
$12
$14
$16
$26
$22
$20
$18
$56
$30
$24
$52
$54
$32
$28
$44
$48
$50
$58
$34
$40
$42
$46
$60
$36
$38
$62
$72
$70
$68
$66
$64
$82
$86
$74
$76
$78
$80
$84
$88
$90
$104
$102
$100
$98
$96
$92
$94
Start!
REVERSE!
Follow the descending order from $104 to $2

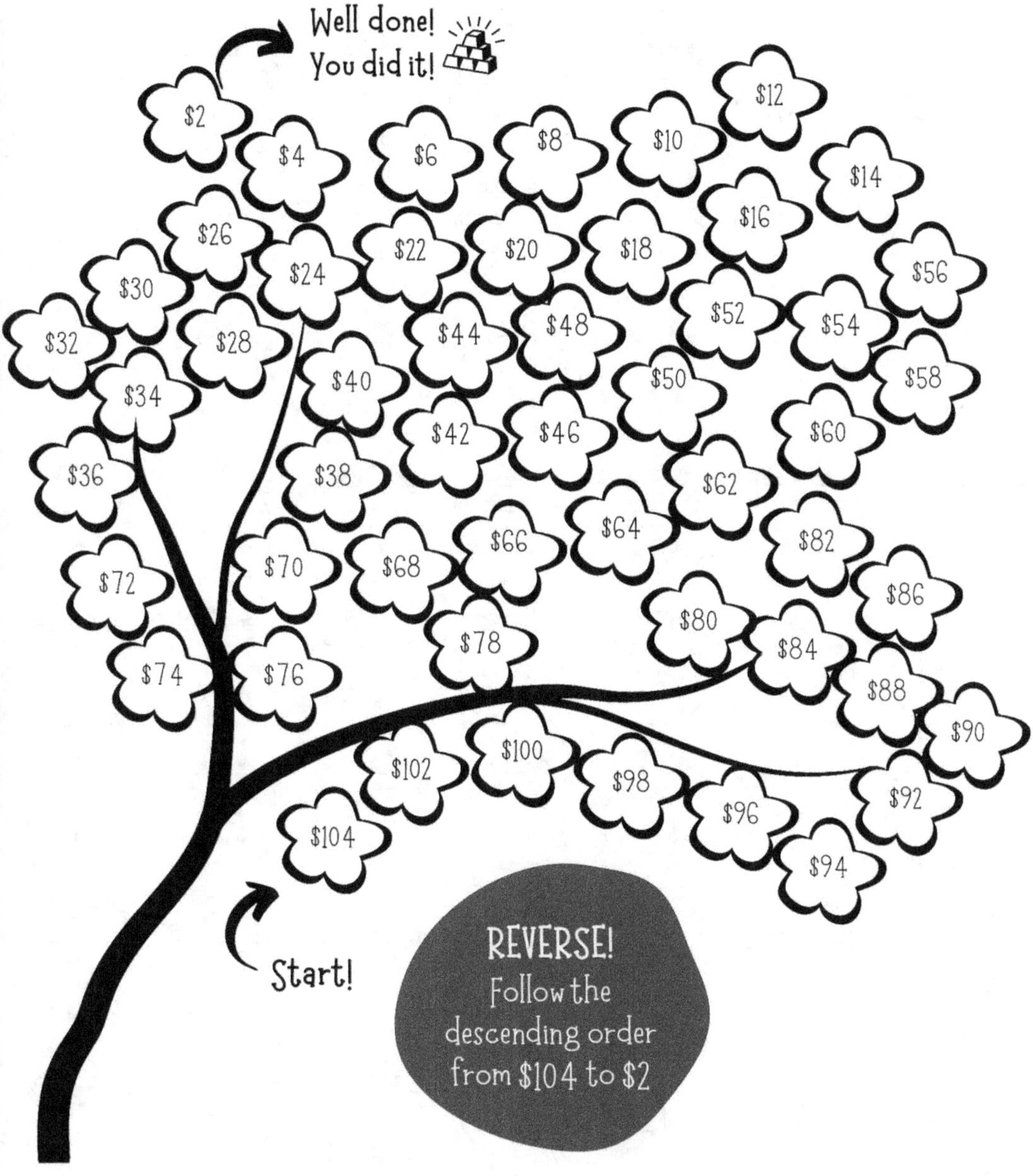

Duration: 52 Weeks
Goal: $2756
Start Date: __________
Finish Date: __________
Start!
$104
$102
$100
$98
$96
$82
$84
$86
$88
$90
$92
$94
$80
$78
$76
$74
$72
$70
$68
$54
$56
$58
$60
$62
$64
$66
$52
$50
$48
$46
$44
$42
$40
$26
$28
$30
$32
$34
$36
$38
$24
$22
$20
$18
$16
$14
$12
Great Job!
$2
$4
$6
$8
$10

Duration: 52 Weeks
Goal: $2000
Start Date: __________
Finish Date: __________

$25
$55
$10
$45
$20
$50
$25
$20
$35
$40
$30
$55
$50
$30
$40
$50
$25
$40
$45
$30
$40
$35
$30
$50
$50
$50
$40
$35
$40
$50
$40
$25
$30
$50
$45
$35
$50
$50
$40
$65
$50
$30
$40
$30
$35
$45
$25
$35
$40
$25
$50
$40
$25
Great job!
You made it!
Start
here!

⏰ Duration: 52 Weeks
🎯 Goal: $2500
🏁 Start Date: __________
🏁 Finish Date: __________

$75 $65 $70 $60 $40 → Wonderful! You did it!

$20 $45 $30 $50 $25 $50 $30

$55 $55 $60 $35 $55 $45 $55

$60 $50 $60 $30 $55 $45 $65

$60 $30 $50 $80 $25 $60 $50

$35 $45 $55 $40 $50 $45 $55

$50 $30 $50 $55 $25 $50 $60

Start here! → $15 $60 $45 $75 $20

Duration: 52 Weeks
Goal: $2500
Start Date: __________
Finish Date: __________
Start!
$15
$50
$30
$55
$35
$20
$55
$60
$45
$50
$25
$45
$60
$50
$30
$75
$45
$55
$50
$80
$40
$50
$60
$45
$55
$25
$60
$30
$65
$55
$45
$30
$25
$50
$60
$60
$20
$50
$45
$55
$30
$35
$50
$60
$55
$40
$50
$55
$70
$65
$60
$75
You made it!

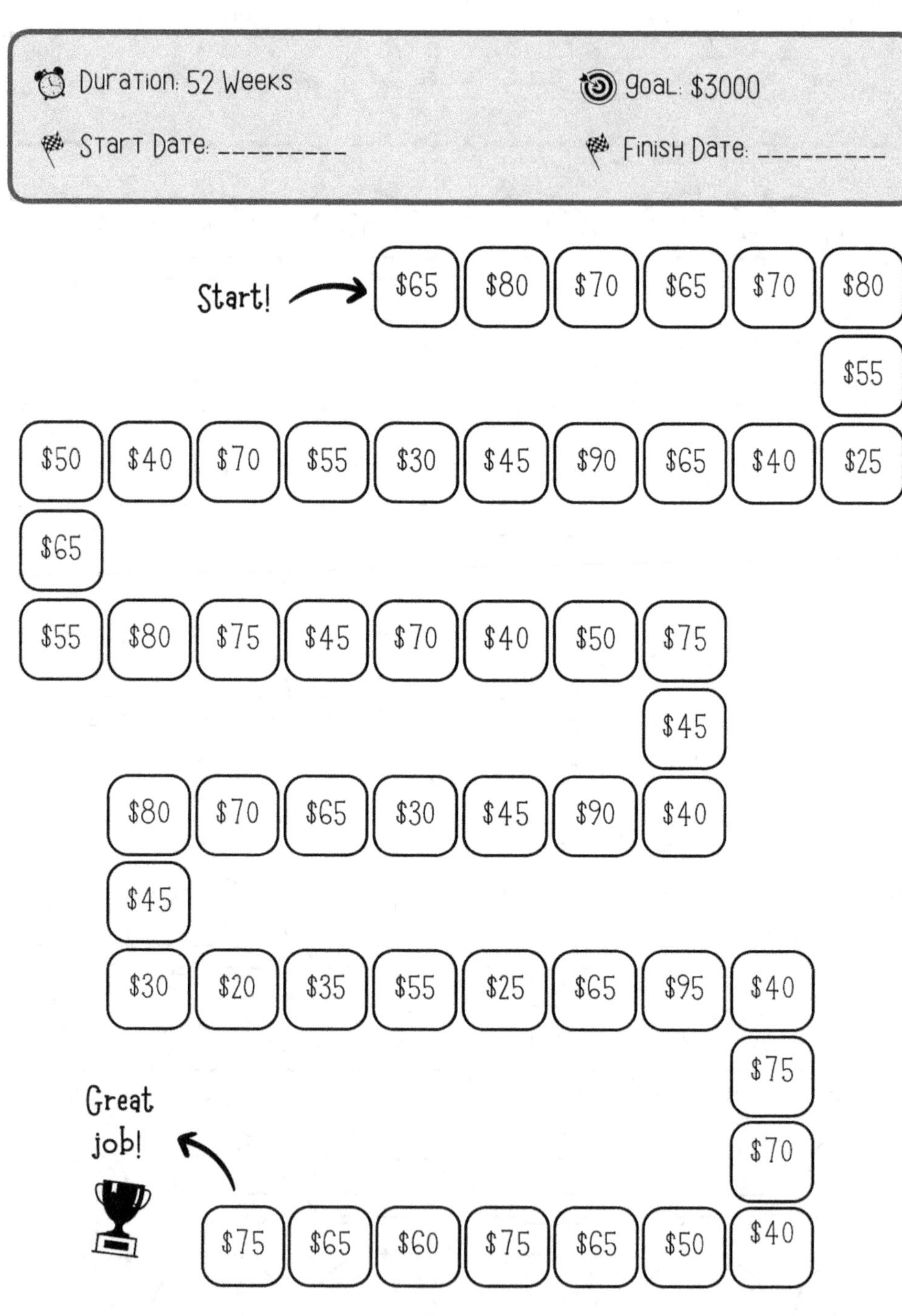

Duration: 52 Weeks
Goal: $3000
Start Date: __________
Finish Date: __________
Start!
$65 $80 $70 $65 $70 $80
$55
$50 $40 $70 $55 $30 $45 $90 $65 $40 $25
$65
$55 $80 $75 $45 $70 $40 $50 $75
$45
$80 $70 $65 $30 $45 $90 $40
$45
$30 $20 $35 $55 $25 $65 $95 $40
$75
$70
Great job!
$75 $65 $60 $75 $65 $50 $40

Excellent!

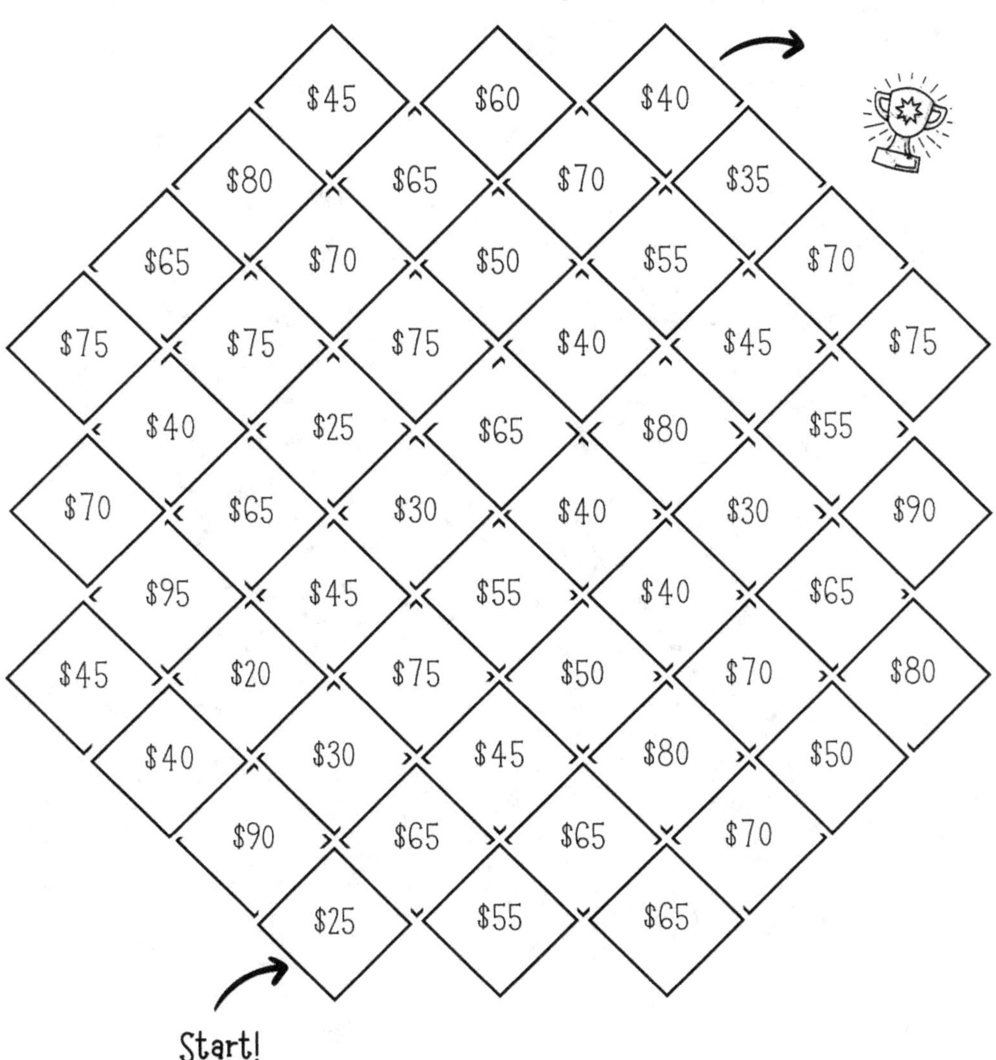

Start!

Duration: 52 Weeks
Start Date: __________
Goal: $5000
Finish Date: __________

$75
$95
$75
$80
Well done!
You did it!
$120
$100
$110
$120
$75
$100
$80
$100
$85
$80
$100
$75
$100
$90
$125
$85
$100
$90
$120
$75
$85
$100
$90
$120
$100
$120
$80
$100
$85
$125
$100
$90
$100
$115
$100
$95
$125
$80
$100
$85
$90
$100
$120
$90
$75
$70
$90
$100
$100
Start!

Duration: 52 Weeks
Goal: $5000
Start Date: __________
Finish Date: __________
Good Work!
$70
$125
$85
$120
$100
$115
$80
$120
$100
$95
$100
$90
$120
$90
$85
$125
$75
$100
$75
$90
$75
$100
$85
$100
$120
$75
$80
$95
$75
$100
$100
$80
$100
$120
$100
$80
$110
$125
$100
$80
$100
$90
$100
$90
$120
$125
$75
$90
$85
$70
$100
$95
Start!

Duration: 52 Weeks

Start Date: __________

Goal: $6000

Finish Date: __________

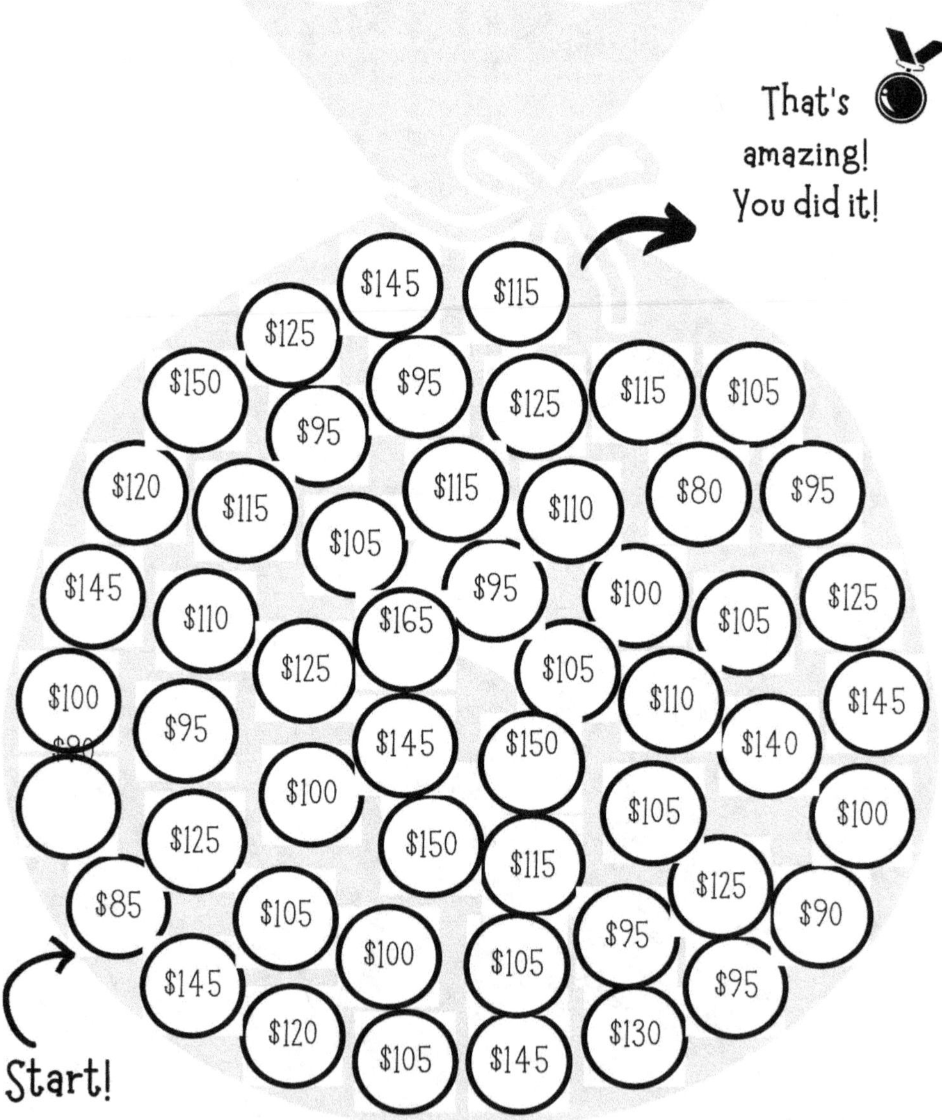

Duration: 52 Weeks
Goal: $6000
Start Date: __________
Finish Date: __________

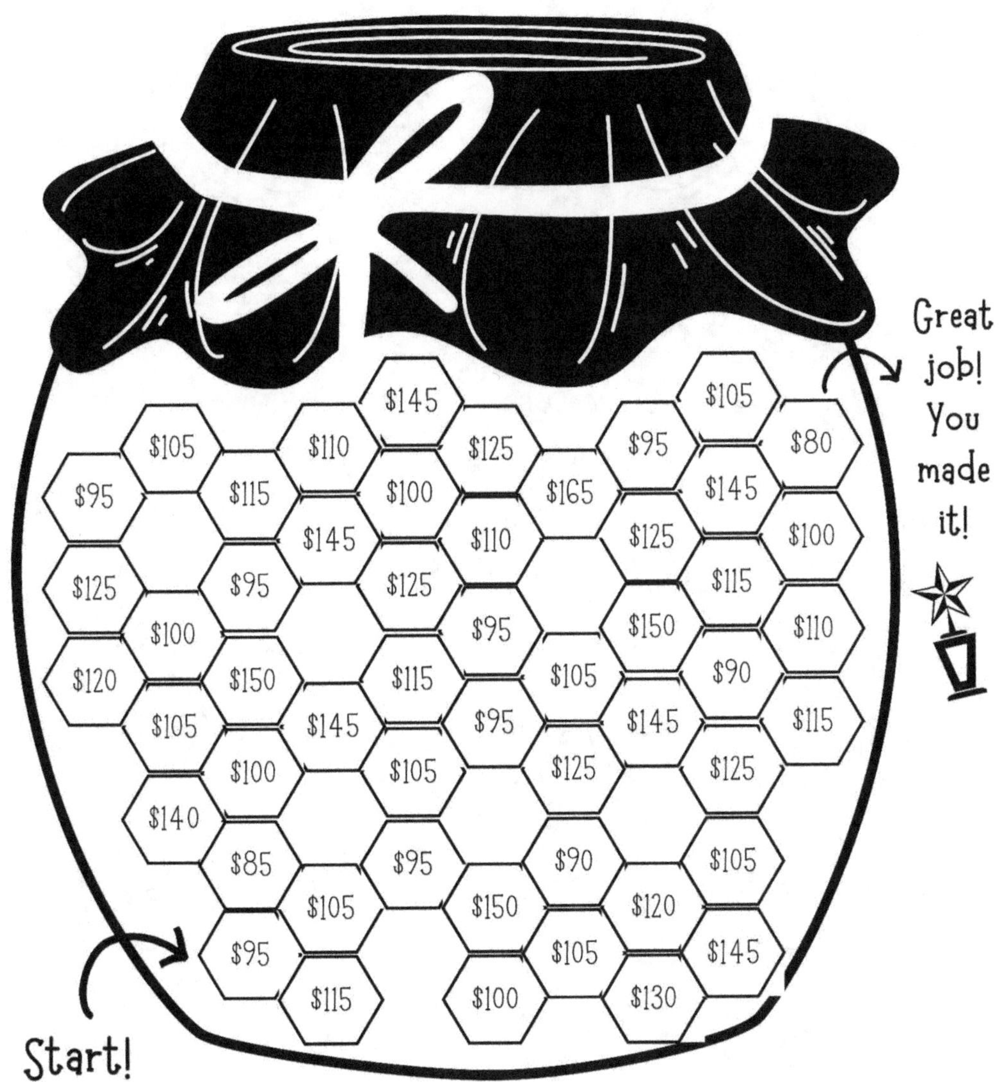

$145
$105
$105
$110
$125
$95
$80
$95
$115
$100
$165
$145
Great job! You made it!
$145
$110
$125
$100
$125
$95
$125
$115
$100
$95
$150
$110
$120
$150
$115
$105
$90
$105
$145
$95
$145
$115
$100
$105
$125
$125
$140
$85
$95
$90
$105
$105
$150
$120
$95
$105
$145
$95
$115
$100
$130
Start!

Duration: 52 Weeks
Goal: $10000
Start Date: __________
Finish Date: __________

$125 $225 $165 $230 $130 $250
Wow! That's impressive!

$245 $220 $120 $200 $150 $240 $245 $215

$160 $225 $240 $170 $220 $130 $245 $220

$230 $145 $190
$245 $155 $235 $210 $165

$225 $155 $215 $240 $200 $160 $230 $100

$145 $200 $155 $215 $200 $240 $125 $220

Start!
$145 $100 $250 $145 $220 $170

Duration: 52 Weeks

Start Date: __________

Goal: $10000

Finish Date: __________

$100
$160
$125
$155
$200
$215

Nice going!
You made
it!

$245
$130
$230
$165
$220
$170
$245
$235

$240
$220
$155
$210
$225
$160
$145
$190

$150
$225
$215
$165
$125
$230
$120
$200

$240
$130
$245
$220
$145
$245
$17.0
$250

$155
$240
$230
$200
$215
$145
$250
$200

Start!

$240
$220
$225
$220
$100
$145

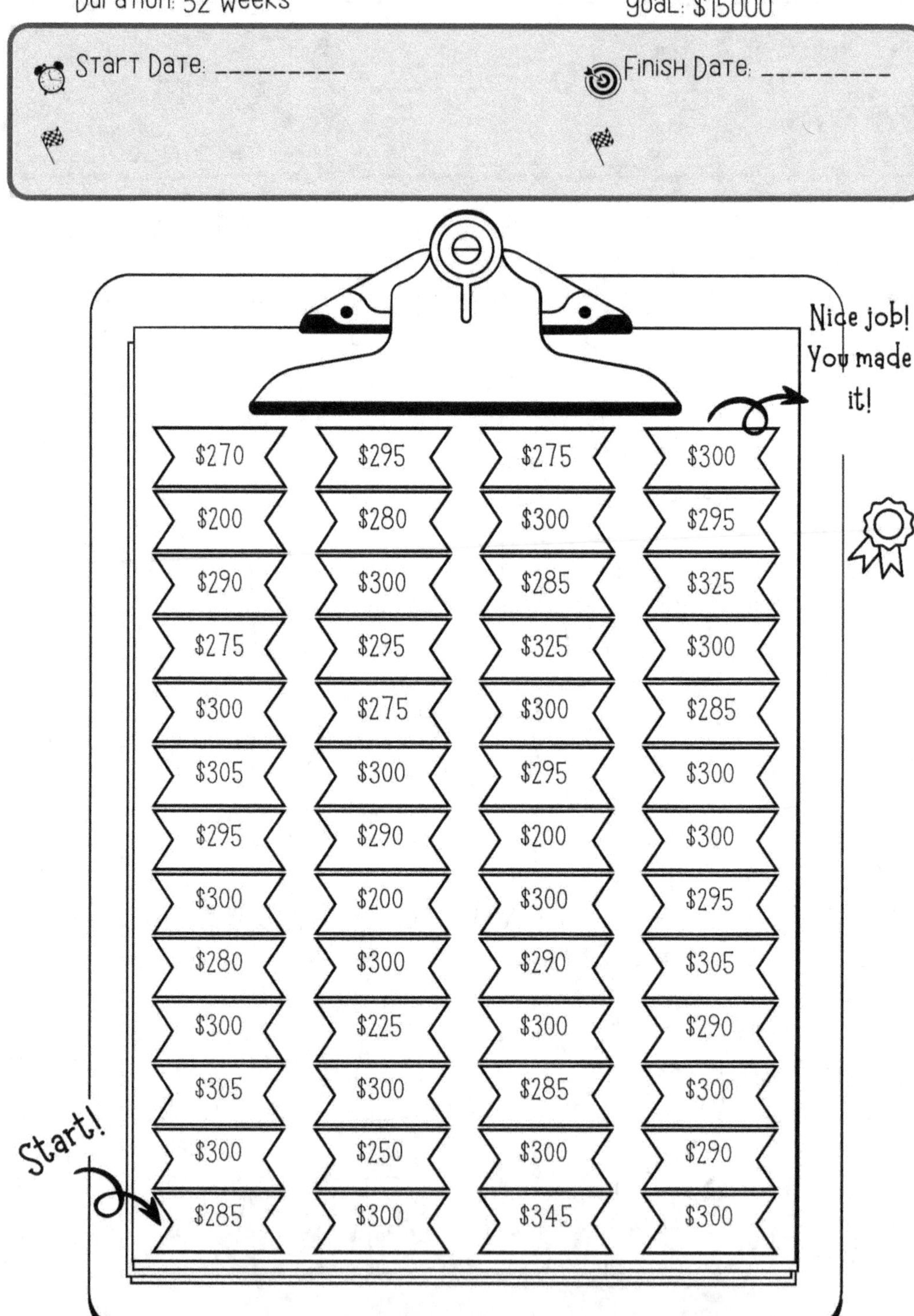

Duration: 52 Weeks
Goal: $15000
Start Date: __________
Finish Date: __________
Nice job! You made it!
Start!
$270 $295 $275 $300
$200 $280 $300 $295
$290 $300 $285 $325
$275 $295 $325 $300
$300 $275 $300 $285
$305 $300 $295 $300
$295 $290 $200 $300
$300 $200 $300 $295
$280 $300 $290 $305
$300 $225 $300 $290
$305 $300 $285 $300
$300 $250 $300 $290
$285 $300 $345 $300

Duration: 52 Weeks
Goal: $15000
Start Date: __________
Finish Date: __________
Start!
$250 $285 $300 $290 $305
$300 $305 $290 $300 $225 $300 $285
$290 $280 $300 $270 $295 $300 $275
$295 $300 $325 $300 $200 $295 $300
$300 $280 $300 $325 $300 $295 $300
$290 $305 $285 $300 $275 $295 $300
$275 $300 $285 $290 $300 $200 $300
Fantastic! You made it!
$345 $300 $295 $300 $200

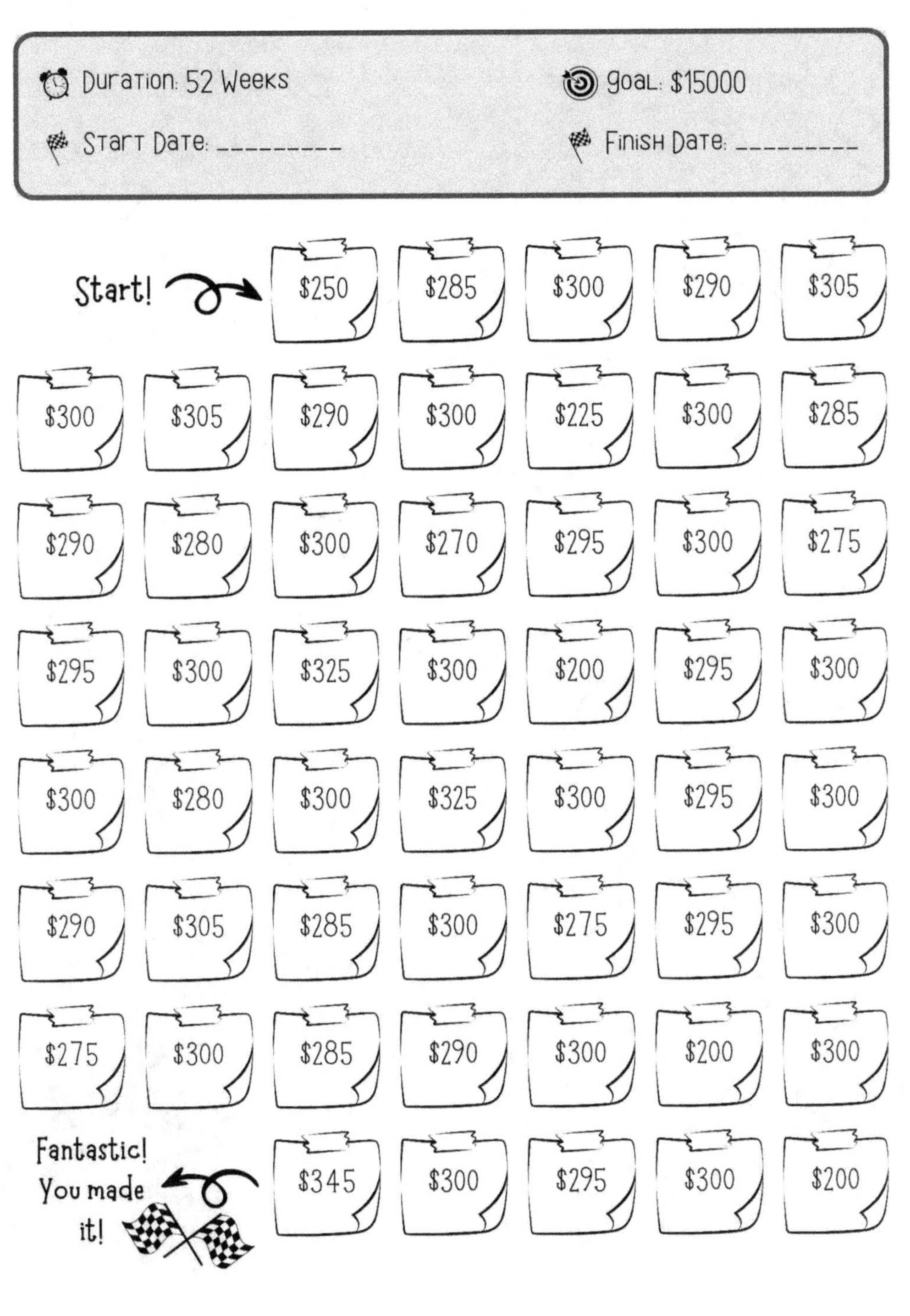

Duration: 52 Weeks
Goal: $20000
Start Date: __________
Finish Date: __________
$500
$310
$240
Start!
$290
$300
$420
$265
$500
$300
$315
$260
$450
$475
$310
$420
$425
$465
$310
$330
$365
$465
$520
$400
$310
$490
$310
$300
$470
$440
$315
$495
$265
$300
$465
$475
$30
$280
$465
$440
$250
$450
$360
Amazing!
$470
$500
$340
$500
$450
$340
$350
$475
$300
$360

Duration: 52 Weeks

Goal: $ ____________

Start Date: __________

Finish Date: __________

Duration: 52 Weeks
Goal: $ ____________
Start Date: __________
Finish Date: __________

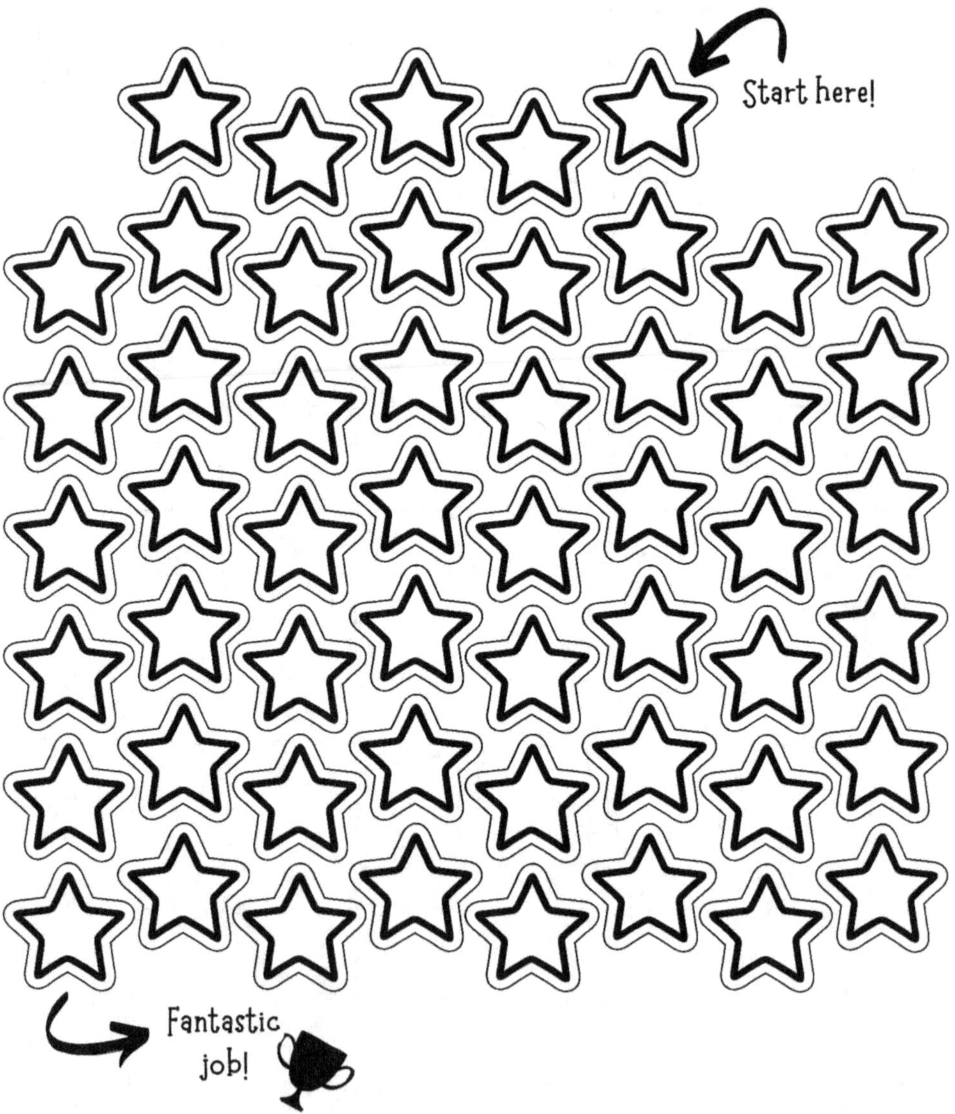

Start here!
Fantastic job!

THANK YOU
THANK YOU
linktr.ee/
CloudIXStudio